TILE STYLE

TILE STYLE

PAINTING & DECORATING
YOUR OWN DESIGNS

Creative ideas for personalizing tiles to
fit any theme, around the home, with
30 step-by-step projects shown in 300
inspirational photographs

MARION ELLIOT

For Iain and Julie Elliot

This edition is published by Aquamarine,
an imprint of Anness Publishing Ltd,
108 Great Russell Street, London WC1B 3NA
info@anness.com

www.aquamarinebooks.com; www.annesspublishing.com

If you like the images in this book and would like to investigate
using them for publishing, promotions or advertising,
please visit our website www.practicalpictures.com for
more information.

Publisher: Joanna Lorenz
Senior Editor: Lindsay Porter
Designer: Lisa Tai
Jacket Design: Adelle Mahoney
Photographer: Adrian Taylor
Stylist: Clare Hunt

A CIP catalogue record for this book is available from the
British Library.

PUBLISHER'S NOTE
Although the advice and information in this book are believed
to be accurate and true at the time of going to press, neither
the authors nor the publisher can accept any legal
responsibility or liability for any errors or omissions that may
have been made nor for any inaccuracies nor for any loss,
harm or injury that comes about from following instructions or
advice in this book.

CONTENTS

INTRODUCTION

 The humble tile, a small piece of fired clay with or without decoration, is a magical material that has been used throughout the ages to enhance, and transform both the interiors and exteriors of our buildings. Tiles have been used to line tombs, cover roofs and make walls and floors for so many centuries that they are an integral part of our architecture – what building does not have some element of tiling in its construction ?

Today tiles continue to be an enduring feature of our lives and can be used in hundreds of stunningly effective ways to disguise, highlight and clad almost every room in the home. They are exciting, vital and amazingly simple to apply and there is no reason to confine their use to the creation of the clinical walls and work surfaces that feature in so many kitchens and bathrooms.

Many cultures, from the Islamic Moors of medieval Spain to the prosperous middle classes of 19th-century Britain and the United States, have used tiles for decorative purposes to dazzling effect. Work such as this can be used as inspiration for ideas to apply to your own home.

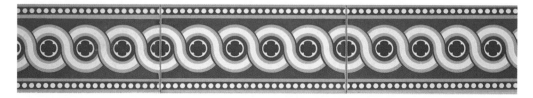

Contained in this book are dozens of exciting tile decorating ideas drawn from many cultures. There are the incredibly ornate Turkish panels of the Ottoman Empire, the flamboyant designs of the Italian Renaissance and the modest encaustic tile designs that can still be seen in the great medieval churches of Europe. Tiles have been a vehicle for just about every design trend, and anything goes. Today there are ranges of cold-set, water-based ceramic paints available. These come in every colour in the spectrum and a variety of finishes and are extremely hard wearing, making tile decoration simple, clean and fun.

If you would rather make the most of the commercial tiles available, then there are lots of creative ideas using plain and patterned tiles to make interesting and dynamic wall coverings. As will quickly become evident elsewhere in this book, the cheapest of tiles can be used

Above: *Tiles from Sintra, Portugal, used here to dramatic visual effect.*

Right: *The Arab Hall of Leighton House, London, built to display the tile collection of Lord Leighton. The ceramicist William de Morgan designed new tiles to complement antique examples.*

to create stylish effects, and basic tiling is so simple and speedy that a room can take on a whole new appearance in just a day. Using tiles en masse is just one option – a single row of tiles can be run around a wall to make a very stylish skirting board (baseboard). Tiles may be patterned, or plain, laid in alternating colours or laid in geometric shapes. Another interesting idea is to apply a block or blocks of patterned and plain tiles to walls to create decorative panels, frames and borders.

If you have kept a box of tile fragments or pieces put them to good use and decorate accessories such as mirror frames and garden planters. Tile mosaic looks wonderful and is a great way to create richly decorative effects using patterns and colours that don't match.

Whatever tiling project you choose to begin with, tiles are wonderfully, infinitely varied and exciting, so start experimenting today.

History of Tiles

Tiles have existed as a form of practical decoration since people have sought to embellish their homes. The development of the tile from small slabs of fired clay to dazzlingly ornate works of art provides a fascinating insight into the history of the decorative arts and how decoration reflects social concerns. From the beautiful mosques of the Ottoman world to the splendid majolica panels of the Italian Renaissance; from blue and white delftware to the hand-crafted designs of William Morris, tiles have reflected the way we live and the way we think about our world. Today we continue to draw inspiration from the designs and innovations of the past to enrich our environment.

History of Decorative Tiles

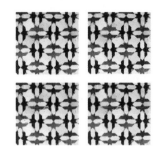

calligraphic inscriptions

ornate decoration

elaborate floors

The tradition of decorative tiles is long and varied, stretching back many centuries and appearing in many different countries and cultures. The urge to decorate that most intimate and personal of spaces, the home, is central to human existence and tiles are an important element.

Historic tiles in museums and books reveal fascinating "snapshots" of what was interesting and important to generations long gone. The social aspirations and religious beliefs of different societies can often be seen in the motifs and symbols depicted on their tiles. Wonderful

calligraphic inscriptions are carved into the tiles that cover the walls of Islamic mosques and palaces, a contrast to the ornate and flamboyantly coloured tiles made by the Italian potters of the Renaissance.

Other historic tiles are decorated with scenes of everyday life, sometimes with popular sports and children's games. The famous blue and white tiles produced in Delft and other Dutch towns still have an endearing liveliness and appeal today, and are widely collected.

Tiles were extremely fashionable in Europe and America in the 19th and early 20th centuries. There

Above: *The Italians used highly decorative majolica tiles to decorate floors, walls and even benches, like this tiled seat from a churchyard in Naples.*

Left: *Tile mosaic clads the walls of the Topkapi Palace in Istanbul. Small pieces of shaped tile are arranged in elaborate patterns to dazzling effect.*

can scarcely be a municipal building, church, grand house or hotel dating from this time that does not have some element of tile decoration, and frequently these buildings are engulfed in tiles of various kinds. The elaborate floors of the Washington Capitol and Westminster Abbey are perfect examples of the importance of decorative tiles in architecture. Many food shops, large and small, chose tiled surfaces because they were perceived as being hygienic and easy to clean as well as attractive — the Food Hall in Harrods, London, is a famous example of a richly tiled interior.

Top: *An amazing tiled stove in a Moscow palace.*

Above: *A detail of the glazed tile frieze that runs around the walls of Michelin House, London, built at the turn of the century to house the Michelin tyre company.*

Left: *Pictorial tile panels were very popular in the late 19th century and were set into walls in public buildings or as fireplace surrounds in domestic interiors.*

Islamic Tiles

Byzantine art

architectural innovation

lustre glazes

The history of glazed tiles begins in Ancient Egypt and the Near East. The first tiles were made by the Babylonians and Assyrians, who were making glazed earthenware bricks to decorate the facades of their buildings around 9000 BC. It is known that glazed tiles were produced in Egypt by 4000 BC. The colour range was limited but the Egyptian potters managed to create beautiful clear blues and greens by adding copper to the glaze.

The potters of the Islamic world, which included Syria, Egypt, Persia, Mesopotamia and Palestine, were responsible for many innovations in tile making and glazing, and their decorative techniques spread via Moorish Spain into Europe. The inventiveness, variety and complexity of their tile decoration drew on their own traditions combined with other stylistic influences, including Byzantine art. The walls of early Islamic buildings such as the Great Mosque of Damascus, built between 705-15 AD, were adorned with magnificent mosaic designs. By the 9th century complicated brickwork patterns and elaborately carved stucco panels were common. The earliest Islamic wall tiles are believed to be those at the Palace of Abbasids in Persia, and tiles had replaced mosaic as the main form of wall decoration in most Islamic countries by the 11th century.

One very important development was the technique of lustre glazes which was introduced to Persia during the 11th century, probably by potters

from Egypt or Mesopotamia. These glazes contained particles of metals, including gold and silver, and were painted on to glazed tiles that had already been fired. The tiles were then fired again at a low temperature to give a sparkling, iridescent effect. Lustre pottery became hugely popular and during the 13th century lustre tiles were distributed throughout Persia for architectural decoration.

Another interesting architectural innovation was the use of glazed bricks and tiles, in a variety of colours, to decorate the exteriors of Islamic buildings. The colours were arranged in complex

Right: *A stunning tile panel from the walls of the Topkapi Palace, Istanbul. Flowers and trees were popular tile motifs.*

Above: *Painted tiles completely cover the walls of this mosque at Esfahan, Iran.*
Below: *A typical example of tile mosaic, with flowing calligraphy and interlocking star design.*

geometric patterns similar to tile mosaic, another visually stunning Islamic invention. In tile mosaic, glazed earthenware slabs were fired and then sawn up into squares, diamonds, stars and triangles. These small tiles were used to build up interlocking patterns on the interior and exterior walls of palaces and mosques. There was great variety in the designs produced and tile mosaic was used throughout Persia during the 13th and 14th centuries on many buildings, including the Blue Mosque of Tabriz.

Tile mosaic, with its small individual tiles, was very labour-intensive but it was popular because otherwise it was very difficult to prevent different-coloured glazes running together during firing if a design was painted on a single large tile. Eventually, however, the potters

of Tabriz developed a new technique in which they divided different areas of the tile with lines of grease, creating a barrier past which the glazes could not run. During firing the grease burned away, leaving a slight gap between the colours.

Some of the best-known Islamic tiles are those made at Iznik in Turkey in the 16th century. The Iznik potters were the first to make tiles with a painted underglaze decoration. Their first tiles were hexagonal, with blue and white decoration, followed by blue and green square and rectangular tiles that together formed large decorative panels. From the mid-16th to the 18th centuries, a vivid crimson was added to their range of colours. A fine example of their work can be seen at the Suleymaniye, built in Istanbul in 1550-57.

Medieval Tiles

interlocking designs

geometric shapes

heraldic imagery

Outside Moorish Spain, tile making did not become established in Europe until the middle of the 12th century. Unlike Islamic tiles, medieval European tiles were nearly always made for floors rather than walls and were used only in churches and palaces. The earliest European tiles were small mosaic tiles, in simple geometric and curved shapes, cut from buff-coloured or red clay and only occasionally glazed. They were used extensively on the floors of cathedrals and abbeys.

At the beginning of the 13th century, Cistercian monks are believed to have been responsible for a radical new technique. Encaustic tiles, as they are known, were decorated by an ingenious process in which a wooden stamp was stamped into the soft, unfired clay tiles. Paler, liquid clay was poured into the recessed areas of the design, creating an inlaid motif that contrasted with the dark background. The tile was then glazed with a transparent glaze. Encaustic tiles were very hardwearing, and many fine floors survive today. The magnificent pavement in the Chapter House at Westminster Abbey, London, boasts heraldic and animal motifs. The Victoria and Albert Museum, London, has fragments of the famous pavement at Chertsey Abbey, Surrey. The production of encaustic tiles fell rapidly after Henry VIII's dissolution of the monasteries. By the time of the Renaissance more elaborate tin-glazed tiles from Spain and Italy were becoming popular throughout Europe.

Right: *These mainly 13th-century tiles in Winchester Cathedral make up the largest and oldest area of floor tiles in England*
Below: *Pale, liquid clay was used to make the heraldic motifs in these tiles from Titchfield Abbey in England.*

The Hispano-Moresque Tradition

intricate tile mosaic

the Alhambra palace

luminous tin glazing

In 711 AD Moorish forces conquered Toledo in Spain, heralding the start of a great era in the decorative arts. The mingling of the two cultures resulted in the rich and varied Hispano-Moresque tradition, which influenced Mediterranean Europe and beyond, developing and refining existing techniques such as tile mosaic. Perhaps the finest example of tile mosaic can be seen today on the walls of the Alhambra Palace, Granada. The palace contains rooms of tiles in an endless variety of interlocking geometric designs. Islamic craftsmen remained in Spain after the 14th century, when the

Below: *Tile panels from the Alhambra Palace, Granada, Spain, the most famous example of the Hispano-Moresque tradition.*

Above: *An elaborate tile panel from Cordoba, Spain.*

Left: *A tiled arched doorway in the Moorish tradition from Toledo, Spain, an important centre of Spanish tile production.*

Below: *Zilij tile borders from Morocco. Zilij is made by a similar process to tile mosaic but the shapes are cut from the clay before firing.*

country had largely returned to Christianity. One of their most important contributions to tile making throughout Europe was tin glazing. Tin oxide added to a lead glaze produced a white opaque glaze after firing, which was an ideal surface for painting on. The Islamic potters also introduced lustre glazes to Spain in the 11th or 12th century, and Valencia in particular was a major centre of production. By the 14th century Valencian tiles depicting portraits and complex patterns were exported all over Europe and created a huge impact, especially in Italy.

Majolica Tiles

Moorish motifs

Renaissance designs

lustre pottery

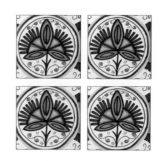

Spanish tiles, were exported to Italy during the 15th century via the island of Majorca. For this reason the work from Spain became known to the Italians as "majolica". The technique of painting metal oxides on top of tin glaze was already known to the Italians, who had been using it to make pottery since the 12th century. However, they had never produced wares as sophisticated as those imported from Spain, and were hugely inspired by lustre pottery with its Moorish-inspired motifs.

Majolicaware was imitated and developed by the Italians, who soon became expert in the technique and were able to produce a sophisticated range of colours including blue, green, yellow, orange, brown

and purple. As well as the wide range of wall plaques, vases and jars they produced, the Italians also made highly decorative, beautifully painted wall and floor tiles in a wide range of Renaissance designs. This instigated the tradition of European painted tiles, which superseded the medieval practice of encaustic tile making.

Majolica was made in several Italian centres: in the 15th century the most famous of these were Tuscany, Faenza and Dureta. In Dureta, tin glazed pottery had been made since the Middle Ages, and it was here that lustre glazes were first used in Italy. During the 16th century Castel Durante, Urbino and Gubbio became important centres of production of majolicaware. At this time, the technique reached its peak of perfection with ambitious, multi-coloured designs featuring biblical scenes, heraldry and commemorative portraiture.

This creative expertise was also applied to tile design and, from the 15th century, ornate and colourful interior and exterior tile pavements, wall tiles and plaques were made in this style. The tiles became very fashionable throughout Europe. As Italian potters migrated to other European countries, the majolica technique spread to Portugal, Spain, France and Flanders. The fashion for wall panels was very influential in the Netherlands, where innovations were to develop.

Left: *The Portuguese embraced tiles wholeheartedly. Examples can be seen throughout the country adorning both private and institutional buildings such as this railway station.*

Left: *A tiled stairway at the Plaza de España, Seville, Spain. Even the bannisters are clad with decoratively painted ceramic.*

Below: *A view of the Plaza de España, built in 1929. The walls are lavishly decorated with majolica tiles painted using traditional techniques.*

Dutch Tiles

Italian potters who migrated to Antwerp, in Flanders, produced majolicaware which included beautiful floor tiles with extravagant Renaissance designs. The Flanders potteries flourished for several years, but on the outbreak of war with Spain the Italian potters moved again to cities such as Rotterdam, Haarlem and Delft.

After the war ended, independence from Spain brought great prosperity to the Netherlands and there was much demand for tiles in new houses. The Italian potters passed on their techniques to the Dutch, who valued the hygienic advantages of tiles and used them to cover the walls and ceilings of kitchens, cellars and dairies. Stoves were also clad with tiles, which helped to radiate heat. Tile panels depicting landscapes and pastoral scenes were spectacular and very popular.

Right: *Dutch tile panels such as this were very popular and were exported throughout Europe.*

Below: *Delftware tiles are a rich source of historical detail, with scenes of everyday life in 17th-century Holland.*

Above: *A charming panel from 17th-century Holland. Vase and flower motifs were especially popular on private and public buildings to decorate house numbers and shop signs.*

With time Dutch taste began to prevail and replaced Italian Renaissance designs. Dutch tiles illustrated scenes and motifs reflecting everyday life. Still lives included vases of tulips or flower pots, while active scenes included children playing, figures skating or fishing or contemporary trades. Other designs such as birds and animals or biblical scenes were popular. The bright colours of Italian tiles were replaced by shades of blue and white, inspired by the Chinese porcelain which came into the Dutch ports and was much admired. Most of the tiles exported abroad came from Delft, so all Dutch tiles became known as Delftware.

Above: *Dutch potters were renowned for their pictorial tile panels, and the images became increasingly sophisticated as this perspectival view of a canal shows.*

English Delftware

During the 17th century, Holland and Flanders cornered the market in tile manufacture and distribution, exporting tiles to the Dutch colonies as well as to Europe. Eventually, Dutch potters obtained royal permission in England to produce Delftware tiles in London.

English potters were trained in the art of Delftware production by their Dutch employers, and a thriving industry in English Delftware was established, spreading to Liverpool and Bristol by the early 18th century. The craze for white china, encouraged by Chinese porcelain imported to Europe, made these products particularly popular.

Initially, all the workshops produced Dutch-style designs, but by the middle of the 18th century English Delftware began to develop a distinctive and recognizable style and a new range of colours and motifs were used in tile production. As English potters became more confident in their skills, they began to produce their own tiles in direct competition with Dutch tile makers. For example, large numbers of tiles with English subject matter executed in a Chinese-inspired style were produced in Bristol. These potteries were also responsible for an innovative from of glaze decoration known as bianco-sopra-bianco (white-on-white) where white motifs painted on to a very light blue background made a slightly raised decoration around tile borders.

The next development in tile production occurred in Liverpool, and was of the greatest significance, for it

Left: *An 18th-century English Delftware tile from Bristol. Initially English potters produced tiles following the Dutch tradition but soon developed their own imagery and interesting glazing innovations.*

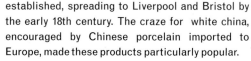

enabled tiles to be mass-produced by a semi-mechanical process. In 1756, John Sadler, whose father was a printer, and Guy Green, one of his employees, registered a process of printing engraved designs on to tin glazed earthenware tiles. Although not the first to experiment with transfer printing, they perfected the technique after several years of investigation.

The tiles used by Sadler and Green were flat and smooth and provided the perfect surface for

Above: *Like their Dutch predecessors, English Delftware potters also produced illustrative tile panels. These could be a relatively simple pattern of as few as four tiles or, as here, 24 or more. This panel depicts St Mary's Church, Redcliffe, Bristol.*

transfer prints. Around this time, porcelain and creamware, a white earthenware pottery developed by Josiah Wedgwood, had become available and Sadler and Green printed a huge number of these at their workshops.

New Mechanization of Tile Production

In the 1830s a revival of interest in decorative tiles was created by a philanthropic wave of church restoration and building by wealthy industrialists, and the Gothic revival in the decorative arts. The taste for floors in the medieval style led to a sudden demand for encaustic tiles, which had not been produced for centuries. Tile-making businesses flourished, notably that of Herbert Minton in Stoke-on-Trent who produced a range of encaustic tiles which were facsimiles of the medieval pavement in Westminster Abbey. Minton also collaborated with the architect A.W.N. Pugin on tile designs for major new buildings such as St Giles Church in Staffordshire, and the Palace of Westminster.

One innovation at this time was pressing slightly moist, powdered clay into tile form using a machine. The invention of the steam-driven press increased production even further. Realizing the importance of tiles in Victorian architecture, Herbert Minton bought a share of the patent for this discovery and also of the patent for lithographic tile printing.

From the 1860s, dozens of tile manufacturers set up in business. Victorian enthusiasm for ceramic tiles was such that huge factories were built, capable of producing vast numbers of tiles. By the 1870s the fashion had spread to America where companies such as the American Encaustic Tile Company, were established.

Right: *A detail of a tiled roof at the Palace of Westminster, London. The architect A.W.N. Pugin designed the decorative details.*

Above: *A transfer-printed English tile, decorated with a Kate Greenaway illustration. The work of well-known artists such as Greenaway and Walter Crane was often transferred to tiles, especially for children's rooms.*

Left: *The Sedilia in St Giles church, Cheadle, Staffordshire. Designed in the Gothic Revival style by A. W.N. Pugin*

Far left: *The tile-clad walls of the Poynter Room, one of three rooms used to serve refreshments at the Victoria and Albert Museum, London. The tile panels depict the seasons and months of the year.*

Private and Public Life

From the 1860s onwards, improved standards of hygiene and greater prosperity led to a great demand for glazed ceramic tiles in Europe and the United States. In England, severe outbreaks of cholera during the middle of the 19th century caused the Victorians to rethink their attitude to hygiene. The rapid growth of cities completely overpowered what few arrangements there had been for the disposal of waste and in 1848 the Public Health act was passed, requiring every home to have fixed sanitary arrangements. By the late 19th century new sewage systems, proper drainage and the hot water circulatory systems were introduced and indoor bathrooms and lavatories began to appear.

Impervious to steam and moisture and easy to keep clean, tiles played an important role in providing a hygienic environment. It was not uncommon to see bathrooms covered floor to ceiling with glazed ceramic tiles, although it was more usual to tile only as far as the dado rail (chair rail). In some bathrooms, tiles were used to make panels behind basins and baths, as today, to

Above: *For sheer exuberance of design it is hard to better the tiled interior of Harrods food hall, London. The tiles raised the concept of hygienic display to an art form.*

Left: *Ornate tiles were widely used to decorate the porches of late 19th-century houses.*

Far left: *A charmingly idealized image of a dairy maid enhances this tile panel from a dairy. Butchers shops, fishmongers and other shops were commonly decorated with panels depicting scenes relevant to the trade.*

Above: *Intricate tessellated pavements made from encaustic tiles were a common sight in the late 19th century.*

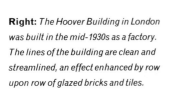

Right: *The Hoover Building in London was built in the mid-1930s as a factory. The lines of the building are clean and streamlined, an effect enhanced by row upon row of glazed bricks and tiles.*

prevent water from damaging the walls. Kitchens and sculleries were treated in the same way, with tiled areas installed for hygienic purposes. Sometimes, kitchen walls were built using glazed bricks, and it became quite common to install tiled panels behind kitchen ranges.

Tiles were used all over the home. The front porches of houses were often beautifully tiled with painted panels, frequently having moulded dadoes with contrasting plain or decorative tiles above. Tiles also featured in hallways to this level. Perhaps the most common decorative use for tiles was a fire surround. Tiles were

eminently suitable for this purpose, being able to withstand direct heat. Many tile manufacturers made the most of this fashion and produced sets of tiles designed to fit within the panels of the fire surround.

By the late 19th century tiles were seen everywhere: adorning municipal buildings, public houses, town halls and shops. One of the most widely seen legacies of this period is the tessellated tile pavement. Thanks to the invention of dust-pressing and semi-mechanical cutting machinery, the small tiles could be made inexpensively, and are still found on pathways, doorsteps and hallways.

New Techniques

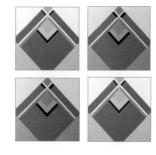

Many tile companies employed artists to create the designs available by the late 19th century, but mass production led to a deterioration in quality. In 1861 William Morris set up Morris, Marshall, Faulkner & Co. to produce hand-crafted furniture, stained glass, wallpaper, furnishing fabrics and hand-painted tiles. Many of the tiles produced were designed by William de Morgan, who hand-painted stunning images of fish, birds, flowers and boats in brilliant colours. De Morgan experimented with the lustre glazes used in the East and perfected an unusual rich ruby red. His tiles had a great impact in North America, where the concept of hand-crafting tiles was enthusiastically embraced. The emphasis of the Arts and Crafts Movement on craftsmanship, also enjoyed a wide-ranging influence.

Tile production in Britain continued into the 20th century, stimulated by the stylized forms of Art Nouveau that swept Europe at the turn of the century. A new tube-lining process meant that tiles with raised outlines could be produced. These were often strong floral designs for distinctive fireplace surrounds. The popularity of decorative tiles in Britain declined dramatically after the First World War but production continued in America until the Depression of the 1930s. The hand-crafting tradition has remained strong, however, and still continues today.

Left: *Stork and fish tiles by William de Morgan. De Morgan's tile designs were lively and bold, and in striking contrast to the mass-produced designs of Victorian times.*

Above: *Four tiles after a design by William Morris. Appalled by the low standards of some mass produced tiles, Morris commissioned beautiful hand-painted designs.*

Left: *A trio of "flower fairy" tiles, after a design by Walter Crane. The tiles are decorated with the raised line technique, where different coloured areas of the design are separated by embossed lines.*

Below: *Four ship tiles, each depicting a different historical design. Clockwise from top left they show an Egyptian galley, a Viking longship, a Phoenician galley and a Tudor galleon.*

American Tiles

studio-based potteries

hand-made traditions

design innovations

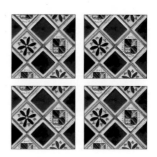

Until the latter half of the 19th century, the United States had no tile industry of its own and was obliged to import tiles from Europe. British tile manufacturers such as Minton established offices in key American ports to feed the demand for domestic tiles. One of the most famous examples of the use of Minton tiles is in the Washington Capitol.

Although tiles were beginning to be made by a few American potteries the industry was given a kick-start in 1876 with the International Centennial Exposition held that year in Philadelphia. A most impressive display of European pottery and tiles was shown, spurring on American ceramicists and convincing them that they could produce tiles to rival those of Europe. Many tile-producing factories were started soon afterwards, mass-producing work that was very similar to European wares.

One such enterprise was the American Encaustic Tile Company, established in 1876 in Zanesville, Ohio. Starting with encaustic floor tiles, it rapidly moved on to produce every type of tile imaginable, becoming a giant of the industry. By the end of the century many tile companies had been established to produce wall and floor tiles. By and large, the

Below: *Tiled fountain at Adamson House, Malibu, California. The tiles were designed by the Malibu Potteries.*

inspired by the Arts and Crafts ethos and produced innovative tiles with matt and semi-opaque glazes. Tiles from Rockwood Pottery were used to decorate part of the New York subway, as were those of the Grueby Faience Company. Some of the most distinctive and beautiful tiles were produced in California and were typified by their bright colours and flamboyant designs, which owed much to Hispanic influences. Perhaps the most famous of the California tile producers was the Malibu Potteries, founded by May Rindge in 1926 and run by outstanding ceramicist Rufus B. Keeler, who had previously owned the California Clay Products Company. The companies both manufactured decorative tiles in a dazzling mixture of geometric and Renaissance-style floral designs that were widely used for California homes. The Malibu Potteries produced tiles for a variety of archictural commissions, most famously for William Randolph Hearst's mansion and the Adamson House, the Malibu home of May Rindge.

Left: *Hearst Castle, San Simeon, California. The tiles were designed by California Faience, circa 1925.*

The Depression of the 1930s decimated the American tile industry and it never really recovered. As in Britain, tiles became functional rather than decorative after the Second World War until the revival of interest in pottery during the 1960s and 1970s. Today, however, the use of tiles in interior and exterior design is deservedly widespread.

American tiles produced by mechanical processes at this time were as uniform as those that were criticized in Britain by William Morris and William de Morgan, although there were some exceptions.

Morris and de Morgan's love of hand-made objects struck a chord with the affluent middle classes who bought their tiles. By the end of the century the influence of the Arts and Crafts Movement had helped to foster an appreciation of the smaller potteries that produced tiles on a more human scale. One of the most influential of all tile producers was Henry Chapman Mercer, founder of the studio-based Moravian Pottery and Tile Works. Other potteries such as Maria Longworth Nichols' Rockwood Pottery of Cincinnati, Ohio, were

Right: *Encaustic floor tiles designed and produced by Minton and Co. for the Senate wing of the United States Capitol Building, Washington, D.C.*

DESIGNING WITH TILES

Whether you are choosing tiles for interior or exterior decoration, it is a good idea to start by considering the space available and your requirements. Is the area too light or dark, large or small? You may want to add splashes of colour to a limited area or cover a larger one with an elaborate pattern. Depending on your taste, you might want to add splendour, cool classicism or Provençal sunshine. Tiles are fairly easy to put up but they are a more permanent wall decoration than paint, so it is important to plan carefully. Experiment with tile samples and colour swatches before committing yourself.

Design Gallery

Above: *You can create an aquatic splashback for a bathroom by mixing plain-coloured wall tiles with patterned tiles and a stencilled border.*

Right: *These contemporary floor tiles create a strong impression, combining hand-painted designs based on the heraldic motifs characteristic of encaustic floor tiles, with borders in dramatic colours.*

Right: *A hand-painted and handmade wall panel from the south of France. Vases of flowers have been a popular and much-used motif in nearly every tile-producing country.*

Below: *Tile friezes and panels have been used to clad walls since the Renaissance and can make a stunning focal point in a garden or courtyard.*

Left: *A tiled floor covered with softly coloured tiles copied from "the Pope's Bedroom" in the Palace of the Popes, Avignon, France. The original floor, laid in the 14th century, was discovered in 1963, having been covered up for hundreds of years.*

Right: *Small glass mosaic tiles have been used to make an abstract panel of colour in a plain wall. The success of the design is due in part to the use of different tones of the same colours.*

Right: *An example of inexpensive everyday tiles being re-invented as a stylish wall covering. These tiles were simply smashed, then reassembled directly on to the wall to make a dynamic and unusual splashback.*

Left: *A "faux" tiled effect has been achieved using squares of sponge to stamp out the design. The lively colours and slightly patchy appearance make a very effective alternative to the real thing.*

Below: *Tiles line the walls of Debenham House, the wildly decorative home built for Sir Ernest Debenham and his family in the first decade of the 20th century.*

Left: *Small glass mosaic tiles have been used to clad this wooden firescreen. The restricted palette and repeat pattern give the design a cool, serene formality.*

Patchwork Ceramic Flooring

Bathrooms, hallways and kitchens are often thought of as utility rooms, and their floorings are correspondingly spartan. But the wide range of ceramic tiles now available enables you to achieve stunning good looks without sacrificing practicality.

Here we chose stylish blue tiles in the same colour range accented by deep indigo. The effect is an irregular patchwork of colour.

MATERIALS

- Pencil and ruler
- Ceramic tiles
- Tile spacers
- Tiling guide, if necessary
- Tile adhesive (waterproof for bathrooms; flexible if on a suspended floor)
- Notched spreader
- Set square (T-square)
- Squeegee
- Grout
- Damp sponge
- Dowel scrap
- Lint-free cloth

1 Find the centre point of the floor by linking the midpoints of opposite walls. Using spacers to allow for grouting, dry-lay rows of tiles out towards the walls to see how many whole tiles will fit and to see whether any need to be cut specially.

2 Spread some adhesive on the floor. As you lay the tiles, use spacers to ensure even gaps between them. Use a set square (T-square) to check that all the tiles are horizontal and level. Use a squeegee to spread grout over and between the tiles.

3 Wipe off the extra grout with a damp sponge before it dries.

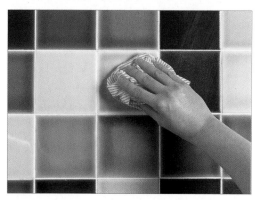

4 Smooth the grout with the piece of dowel, then polish with a dry, lint-free cloth when the grout has dried.

Work Surface

This cheerful work surface or table top is a good way to use up an odd assortment of left-over tiles. The vibrant mix of colours creates the mood of a Mediterranean café. Because the tiles are not exactly the same size the spacing and grouting are judged by eye, but a little unevenness will add to the rustic charm! Tiles for work surfaces need to be at least 6 mm (¼ in) thick to withstand heat, so normal wall tiles are not suitable. Choose tiles that are not too highly glazed, otherwise they will be very slippery and impractical to work on. Make sure the kitchen unit or table will bear the weight of the tiles by adding extra supports and strengthening the joints.

MATERIALS

- Tape measure
- Protective face mask
- Saw
- Workbench and clamps
- Waterproof plywood 16 mm (⅝ in) thick or chipboard 20 mm (¾ in) thick
- PVA (white) glue and brush
- Selection of ceramic tiles
- Pencil (optional)
- 4 mm (³⁄₁₆ in) battens
- Panel pins (tacks)
- Tack hammer
- Rubber gloves
- Flexible waterproof tile adhesive
- Notched spreader
- Sponge
- Ready-mixed grout (for table top) or epoxy grout (for work surface)
- Lint-free cloth

1 Measure your work unit or tabletop. Wearing a face mask, cut a piece of waterproof plywood or chipboard to fit. Seal both sides with PVA (white) glue and leave to dry.

2 Lay the tiles on the board and work out the design. If you need to cut tiles to fit, find the centre of the board first and calculate the number of whole tiles. Draw a box around this area.

3 Wearing a face mask, cut the battens into four strips. Using panel pins (tacks), attach a strip to each side of the board so that they protrude above the edge to form a lip the same depth as the tiles.

4 Wearing rubber gloves, spread tile adhesive over about a 60 cm (24 in) square of the board. (If you need to cut tiles, start within the marked box.) Key (scuff) the surface of the adhesive using the notched edge of the spreader.

5 Carefully position the tiles on the board, judging the grouting distance by eye. If necessary, cut tiles to fit (see Basic Techniques). When the whole board has been tiled, remove excess adhesive with a damp sponge. Leave to set.

6 Apply the grout, following the manufacturer's instructions. Remove excess grout with a damp sponge, then polish the tiles with a dry, lint-free cloth.

Window Recess

Tiling a small area of a room will focus attention and add colour and pattern without being overpowering. Here, two different designs of hand-painted tiles have been used to accentuate a window recess, the colours complementing the bright-coloured wall.

For a completely different effect, plain terracotta tiles with a curved edge would give a Mediterranean look to the window. Plain, matt-glazed tiles in rich shades of blue would create a very different note of Moorish magnificence.

MATERIALS

- Protective face mask
- Gloves
- Medium-grade sandpaper
- Rubber gloves
- Tile adhesive and powdered grout (or all-in-one tile adhesive and grout)
- Notched spreader
- Sponge
- 10 x 10 cm (4 x 4 in) hand-painted earthenware tiles, in two designs
- Masking tape
- Lint-free cloth

1 Wearing a face mask and gloves, sand the paintwork on the window sill and walls to remove any loose paint. Key (scuff) the surface.

2 Wearing rubber gloves, spread a thick layer of tile adhesive in one corner of the window. Using a damp sponge, remove any adhesive that gets on to the wall.

3 Using the notched edge of the spreader, key the surface only halfway through, leaving a thick layer of adhesive.

4 Place the first two tiles in position on the wall, butting them closely together and lining up the outside edge of the outer tile with the edge of the wall. Hold the tiles in place with masking tape until set.

5 Spread adhesive in the opposite corner of the window and key as before. Position two vertical tiles as in step 4. Lay tiles along the sill, overlapping the edges of the vertical tiles.

6 Spread adhesive up the sides of the window frame and key. Position the contrasting tiles, lining up the edges. Tape in place as before until set. Grout all the tiles, removing any excess with a damp sponge. Polish with a dry, lint-free cloth.

Vinyl Floor Tiles

Unlike ceramic tiles, vinyl tiles are very easy to cut and are thus ideal for creating an endless number of designs. This formal star motif is a bright-coloured modern version of the tessellated floors popular in Victorian hallways.

Some vinyl tiles are self-adhesive, others are attached using special tile adhesive, as here. Work in a well-ventilated room and if the adhesive is solvent-based, wear a protective face mask. Vinyl tiles must be laid on a smooth surface such as hardboard, and should not be laid directly on to the floor itself.

MATERIALS

- Squared graph paper
- Coloured pencils or pens
- Sealed vinyl tiles, in appropriate colours
- Pencil
- Long metal ruler
- Cutting mat
- Craft knife
- Set square (T-square)
- Rubber gloves
- Vinyl tile adhesive
- Rubber-edged spreader
- Wooden roller

1 Work out the dimensions of your design on graph paper. The star design is the same dimensions as a single vinyl tile. Using a pencil and a metal ruler draw multiples of each pattern piece on the appropriate coloured tiles.

2 Place each tile on a cutting mat. Using a craft knife and metal ruler, carefully score once along the pencil lines. When all the lines have been scored, simply snap off the pieces. Make separate piles of each shape.

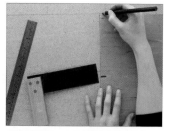

3 Measure the room, find the centre and mark with a cross on the hardboard floor. Carefully centre a tile over the cross and mark a square to outline it. Using a set square (T-square) and ruler, mark out a grid across the whole room.

4 Arrange the tile pieces to make one complete star pattern. Wearing rubber gloves and working with plenty of ventilation, spread a thin coat of vinyl tile adhesive over the centre square.

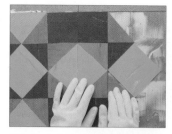

5 Starting in the top right-hand corner of the square, press each piece of the design into place so that they butt up tightly together. Use the set square constantly to check that the design is straight.

6 Continue to tile the floor a square at a time. Using a wooden roller, apply even pressure over the surface to help bond the tile pieces to the hardboard.

Moroccan-style Splashback

Shades of blue and ivory Venetian glass tiles make a lovely cool splashback for a bathroom sink. They are arranged here in a simple geometric design, but you can experiment with other patterns — position the tiles diagonally to make a diamond shape, or use alternate coloured squares like a chequerboard. For a co-ordinated look, use one of the tile colours to make a thin border around the bath or repeat the design on the door of a bathroom cupboard. You could also continue the design around a window.

MATERIALS
- Craft knife
- 1 cm (½ in) thick waterproof MDF (medium-density fibreboard), chipboard or plywood
- PVA (white) glue and brush
- Venetian glass tiles
- Pen
- Workbench and clamps
- Hand drill
- Plastic drinking straw
- Rubber gloves
- All-in-one flexible waterproof tile adhesive and grout
- Notched spreader
- Sponge· Lint-free cloth
- Yacht varnish and brush

1 Using a craft knife, score the surface of the board or plywood to provide a key (scuffed surface) for the tiles.

2 Seal both sides with diluted PVA (white) glue to prevent it from warping.

3 Plan the design on the board. Mark a point in each corner for the screw holes, for hanging the splashback on the wall.

4 Clamp the board firmly and drill the screw holes. Put a drinking straw in each hole to keep them open. Wearing rubber gloves, spread tile adhesive over about one-third of the board.

5 Position the tiles on the board, pressing them firmly into the adhesive. Repeat over the rest of the board, working on one-third at a time. Remove excess adhesive with a damp sponge. Leave to dry.

6 Spread grout over the surface of the tiles, taking care not to dislodge them. Remove excess with a damp sponge, then polish with a dry, lint-free cloth. Seal the back with 2 coats of yacht varnish.

Framed Tile Pictures

There are so many beautiful, extraordinary tiles available that you may be loath to set a current favourite permanently into the wall for fear there may be a design you like more just around the corner. Here is the perfect solution: box frames containing a constantly changing display of tiles that can be hung anywhere as the fancy takes you. The backing boards can be repainted in minutes. Foam pads are used to hold the tiles in place inside the frames. Use those intended for outdoors, if you are going to hang the tiles in a damp environment such as the bathroom.

MATERIALS

- Box frame deep enough to comfortably contain a tile
- Diluted PVA (white) glue and glue brush
- Emulsion (latex) paint
- Medium paintbrush
- Set square (T-square)
- Ruler
- Pencil
- Exterior-strength sticky fixing pads
- Tile
- Tack hammer
- Panel pins (tacks)

1 Seal the surface of the hardboard backing of the frame using diluted PVA (white) glue. Leave the backing to dry thoroughly.

2 Paint the backing board with emulsion paint (latex) in the colour of your choice. You may need more than one coat to achieve a good, even surface. Leave the backing board to dry.

3 Using a set square (T-square) and ruler, find the centre of the backing board and mark the point with a cross.

4 Place a sticky pad in each corner of the tile. Press the pads firmly in place and remove the backing paper.

5 Centre the tile over the cross in the middle of the backing board. When you are satisfied that the tile is in the right position, press it in place.

6 Place the frame face down. Position the board over the back of the frame and attach it, using small panel pins (tacks).

Checked Tiles

If you have your heart set on a particular tile but find it is outside your budget, do not despair; it is possible to create quite dramatic results with the cheapest of tiles as long as you use them imaginatively. Here, basic wall tiles in two shades of blue have been used to create a stunning chequerboard effect that is topped with a thin, decorative band of tile strips. The strips make a visual "dado rail" (chair rail) that divides the tiles' surface quite naturally into two distinct areas. The upper portion of the wall is then finished using lighter blue tiles.

MATERIALS

- Wooden battens
- Hammer
- Nails
- Spirit level (carpenter's level)
- Set square (T-square)
- Rubber gloves
- All-in-one tile adhesive and grout
- Notched spreader
- 15 x 15 cm (6 x 6 in) tiles in light and dark colours
- Tile spacers
- Protective goggles
- Protective leather gloves
- Tile cutter
- Sponge
- Lint-free cloth

1 Prepare the wall properly (see Basic Techniques), then fix up a pair of batten guides at right angles where the first row of tiles will start (see Basic Techniques).

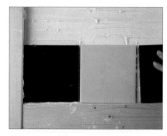

2 Wearing rubber gloves, spread tile adhesive over an area approximately 60 cm (24 in) square. Use the notched spreader to key (scuff) the surface. Set in the tiles with alternating light and dark.

3 When you have laid as many alternating tiles as you want, cut 5 cm (2 in) strips of the darker tiles. Apply and key the tile adhesive as before, then set the strips in position using tile spacers.

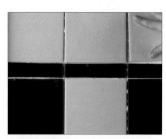

4 Lay the light coloured tiles in place above the border, using tile spacers as before. Cut any tiles you need to complete the edges and set them in place. Use a damp sponge to remove any excess adhesive and leave the tiles to dry.

5 When the tiles are dry, grout them thoroughly, wearing rubber gloves. Press the grout down into the gaps between the tiles.

6 Remove any excess grout using a damp sponge and leave the tiles to dry. When the grout is dry, polish the surface of the tiles with a dry, lint-free cloth.

Door Panel

During the Victorian era, tiles were used to decorate all types of domestic objects, from fireplace surrounds to furniture. This idea has been adapted from the Victorian use of decorative panels to brighten up traditional interior doors. Once grouted, the edges of the tiles are encased with strips of thin wooden moulding. This provides a neat finish, echoing the design of the door panels, and helps to keep the tiles in place. Remember that tiles will make the door heavy, so the idea is not suitable for a child's room. Before you proceed, check that the door hinges are firmly attached and reinforce them if necessary.

MATERIALS

- Protective mask
- Protective leather gloves
- Medium-grade sandpaper
- Craft knife
- Rubber gloves
- Flexible waterproof tile adhesive
- Notched spreader
- 2 decorative wall tile panels
- Plain wall tiles in complementary colours
- Tile spacers (optional)
- Damp sponge
- Ready-mixed grout
- Rubber-edged spreader
- Lint-free cloth
- Strips of recessed wooden moulding
- Saw
- Mitring block
- Tack hammer
- Panel pins (tacks)

1 Wearing a protective mask and gloves, prepare the surface of the door panels by rubbing them down with sandpaper.

2 Once the door is sanded, use a craft knife to score the panels, creating a key (scuffed surface) for the tile adhesive.

3 Wearing rubber gloves, spread a generous layer of flexible tile adhesive over the surface of the first door panel.

4 Using the notched spreader, key (scuff) the surface of the adhesive to ensure good adhesion for the tiles.

5 Position the tiles in order on the panel, using tile spacers if necessary. Remove excess adhesive using a damp sponge. Repeat the process to apply tiles to the other panels. Leave the adhesive to dry.

6 Grout the tiles. Remove the excess grout using a damp sponge and polish the tiles using a dry, lint-free cloth. Wearing a protective mask, cut strips of recessed moulding to fit around the panels, mitring the edges. Hammer the moulding in position using panel pins (tacks).

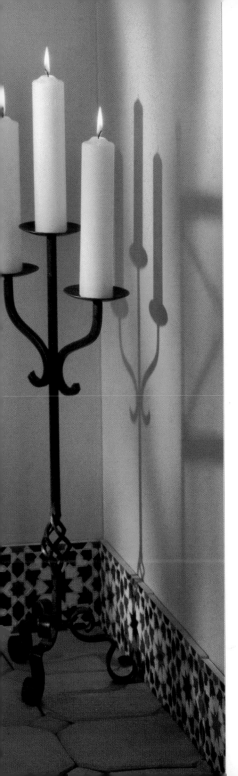

Spanish Border

These long, star-studded Spanish tiles are a modern version of the tiles made by medieval Islamic potters. They were widely used in place of the more time-consuming tile mosaics which decorate buildings such as the Alhambra Palace in Granada. Tiles with interconnecting patterns look wonderful as an all-over wall decoration. Here they are used to add a touch of Spanish style in a simple border along the base of a wall.

MATERIALS

- Ruler
- Spanish tiles
- Pencil
- Set square (T-square)
- Rubber gloves
- All-in-one tile
  adhesive and grout
- Notched spreader
- Tile spacers (optional)
- Sponge
- Lint-free cloth

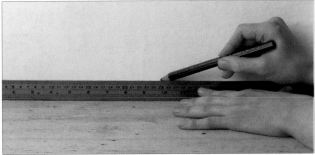

1 Measure the length of one tile. Using a pencil, mark the wall into sections of this measurement.

2 Using a set square (T-square), draw a vertical line at each mark to help position the tiles accurately.

3 Wearing rubber gloves, spread a thick layer of tile adhesive on the wall. Cover enough wall to apply four or five tiles at a time.

4 Using the notched edge of the spreader, key (scuff) the surface only halfway through, leaving a thick layer of adhesive.

5 Slide each tile into position. You may wish to use tile spacers or you could space them by eye.

6 Wipe the surface of the tiles and the wall with a damp sponge to remove any excess adhesive. Leave to dry.

7 Grout the tiles thoroughly, pushing the grout down well into the gaps between the tiles.

8 Using a damp sponge, remove any excess grout. Leave to dry. Polish the surface of the tiles with a dry, lint-free cloth.

Floral Wall Panel

Flowers have always been a popular theme for tiled wall panels, from the ornate vases of flowers produced at the Iznik potteries in Ottoman Turkey to the blue and white tulip panels made by Delft potters in Holland. Flowers are also a recurring theme in folk art in many countries.

These handmade and hand-painted tiles from the South of France are set directly on to the wall. A border of plain tiles in toning colours makes a perfect frame for the design.

MATERIALS

- Protective face mask
- Protective gloves
- Medium-grade sandpaper
- Battens
- Plumbline
- Set square (T-square)
- Hammer
- Nails
- Rubber gloves
- All-in-one waterproof tile adhesive and grout
- Notched spreader
- Plain handmade tiles, in various colours
- Tile spacers (optional)
- Handmade, hand-painted floral tile panel
- Sponge
- Lint-free cloth

1 Prepare the surface of the wall thoroughly (see Basic Techniques). Decide the position of the panel, then fix two guide battens to the wall (see Basic Techniques).

2 Wearing rubber gloves, spread a layer of tile adhesive over the wall between the battens.

3 Using the notched edge of the spreader, key (scuff) the surface of the adhesive.

4 Start to build up the bottom and side of the border with plain tiles. Use tile spacers or space the tiles by eye.

5 Begin to fill in the space between the bottom and side of the border with the floral tile panel. Continue to build up the panel and border gradually, moving diagonally from the starting point and making sure that the floral panel pieces are properly aligned. Remove excess adhesive with a damp sponge. Leave to dry overnight.

6 Wearing rubber gloves, grout the tiles, pushing the grout down well into the gaps between the tiles. When the grout has set slightly, remove the excess with a damp sponge. When completely dry, polish with a dry, lint-free cloth.

DECORATING TILES

Historic tiles in museums and books provide an endless source of ideas and inspiration. If you are fortunate enough to visit Istanbul in Turkey or Granada in Spain, you will see some of these wonderful decorative tiles in situ. Use these and other designs as sources of inspiration when you are planning to create your own tiles. Consider single motifs or recurring patterns as tiles can be self-contained and used as a single focal point, or elaborately designed and part of a larger panel. you can paint, stamp, stencil or print a design on to tiles. Other inventive techniques include using tube-lining, air-drying clay or shells and other objects to create low-relief decoration.

Design Gallery

Left: *These bold, humorous tiles are decorated in a painterly style using onglaze enamels. They are a perfect example of the fusion of contemporary illustration and tile production that stretches back to the early 19th century.*

Above: *The bold, graphic designs on these small tiles bring the art of encaustic tile making into the 20th century. However, the simplicity and directness of the tiles is still very much in tune with the tiles of the Middle Ages.*

Left: *These cheerful sunflower tiles have a jaunty Mediterranean feel. They are teamed with slightly aged tiles in rich colours to stunning effect.*

Left: *These tiles are painted with a loose, luscious lemon design. The surrounding leaves form an all-over design that allows the tiles to be positioned in a variety of combinations.*

Right: *This delightful cherub design was painted with cold-set ceramic enamels using colours characteristic of majolicaware.*

Left: *These tiles have been stencilled with a bold fleur-de-lys motif and are inspired by the wonderful encaustic floor tiles found in medieval churches.*

Above: *Metal leaf and hand-coloured engravings are an unusual and sumptuous treatment for wall tiles.*

Right: *A single tile with a strong design can be used as a wall plaque in the garden or in the kitchen to protect surfaces from hot dishes. Here, the design was shaped into the clay before firing.*

Blue Wave Tiles

This striking wave design is done with a stencil cut from corrugated card (cardboard). Make sure the outer edges of the stencil match so that the repeat runs smoothly across the tiles. Different shades of paint are spattered over the tiles with an old toothbrush to give the effect of sea spray. Protect your work surface, and wear old clothes, a face mask and goggles for this technique as the paint can get everywhere! These tiles are perfect for a bathroom, teamed with rope, driftwood and shell accessories.

MATERIALS

- Scrap paper
- Pencil
- Thin corrugated card (cardboard)
- Craft knife
- Cutting mat
- Non-toxic, water-based, cold-set ceramic paints: light blue, mid-blue and gold
- Old saucers
- Protective face mask
- Safety goggles
- Old toothbrush
- Scraps of stiff card
- Plain white glazed ceramic tiles

1 Draw a wave motif on to scrap paper, and transfer on to corrugated card (cardboard) (see Basic Techniques). Cut out the stencil, using a craft knife and cutting mat.

2 Dilute some light blue paint in a saucer. Wearing a face mask and goggles, dip the tooth-brush in the paint. Using a small piece of stiff card, comb the bristles towards you, spattering paint over the tile. Leave to dry.

3 Place the wave stencil on the tile. Dilute some mid-blue paint in another saucer. Spatter over the tile as before. Remove the stencil and leave to dry thoroughly.

4 Finally, dilute gold paint in a saucer and spatter lightly over the whole surface of the tile to add extra depth to the design.

Chevron Patterned Tiles

These bold tiles make an interesting geometric repeat design, which can be arranged in different ways to create a variety of patterns. Make sure the diagonal lines match exactly from tile to tile. Simple geometric patterns can be very powerful, so lay the tiles out first to judge the effect before you fix them in place. The chevron motif is reminiscent of the medieval heraldic designs worn on the shields of knights in armour. The brown and off-white colour scheme would team beautifully with terracotta floor tiles and distressed wooden furniture for a rustic effect.

MATERIALS

- Masking tape
- Scissors
- Plain white glazed ceramic tiles
- Set square (T-square)
- Non-toxic, water-based, cold-set ceramic paints: brown and cream
- Old saucers
- Open-textured natural or man-made sponge
- Small paintbrush

1 Lay strips of masking tape diagonally across the tile, as shown, to divide it into stripes. Use a set square (T-square) to check the lines are straight.

2 Pour a little brown paint into a saucer. Using a sponge, apply the paint between the strips of masking tape. Apply the paint lightly to give a mottled effect.

3 When the paint is dry, carefully peel off the tape.

4 Using a small paintbrush, fill in the remaining areas of the tile with cream paint.

Alphabet Tiles

Children will love these chunky letter tiles. Use them to make a panel or a frieze around a bedroom or playroom wall, mixing the letters at random or spelling out a name. If you prefer, you can paint the tiles in bright colours. For a child's room it is especially important to use non-toxic ceramic paints.

MATERIALS

- Fine black marker pen
- Plain white glazed ceramic tiles
- Fine and medium paintbrushes
- Black non-toxic, water-based, cold-set ceramic paint
- Old saucer

1 Using a fine marker pen, draw the outline of the letter on to the tile, extending the lines right to the edges of the tile.

2 Using a fine paintbrush, go over the outlines with black paint. Leave to dry.

3 Using a medium paintbrush, paint bold black stripes down one side of the tile.

4 Leaving the letter white, fill in the rest of the design with dots, spots and fine lines. Leave to dry thoroughly.

Roman Numeral Tiles

The elegance of Roman numerals is classical and timeless and is used to great effect in this striking design. Assemble these tiles in a random design to make a stylish splashback in a bathroom or a frieze around a door frame. Alternatively, you can use them to make up a particular number or date, such as the year your house was built or the date of a wedding. The tiles are stencilled in blue paint on a white background, but you can use any colour combination to fit in with your existing colour scheme.

MATERIALS

- Scissors
- Scrap paper
- Oiled stencil card (cardboard)
- Plain white glazed ceramic tiles
- Metal ruler
- Pencil
- Cutting mat
- Craft knife
- Small stencil brush
- Blue non-toxic, water-based, cold-set ceramic paint
- Protective face mask
- Spray ceramic varnish

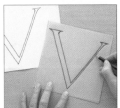

1 Cut a piece of scrap paper and a piece of stencil card (cardboard) the same size as the tile. Using a ruler, draw the numeral. Transfer the numeral on to the stencil card (see Basic Techniques).

2 Place the stencil card on a cutting mat. Using a craft knife, carefully cut away the card inside the pencil lines.

3 Lay the stencil on the tile, aligning the corners. Using a small stencil brush, stipple blue paint on to the tile. Don't overload the brush, and remove excess paint before each application. Leave to dry.

4 In a well-ventilated area, place the tile on a sheet of waste paper. Wearing a face mask and holding the can about 30 cm (12 in) from the tile, spray it with an even coat of ceramic varnish.

Mexican Folk Art Tiles

1 Using a soft pencil, draw a simple flower and spotted border design on the tile.

2 Fill in the petals, using a medium-sized paintbrush. Add a dot of contrasting paint for the flower centre.

3 Paint the border in a dark colour, leaving the spots blank.

4 Using a fine paintbrush, paint small multicoloured spots in the centre of each blank spot. Leave to dry.

These cheerful tiles are based on the simple, naive designs popular in Mexico. The hand-painted motifs are easy to do so you can build up a set of tiles quite quickly. They would add a colourful touch to a kitchen wall, as an all-over design or a border. These tiles also work well used individually to give occasional focal points in a wall of plain tiles. Paint the tiles in traditional rich, deep colours, as illustrated here, or choose tones to match your own colour scheme.

MATERIALS

- Soft pencil
- Off-white glazed ceramic tiles
- Medium and fine paintbrushes
- Non-toxic, water-based, cold-set ceramic paints
- Old plate

Tartan Tiles

Tartan designs have been popular in interior design since the Victorian era. There are many traditional tartans to inspire you or you can invent your own colour scheme, as here. Shades of a single primary colour give a very subtle effect, or you could create a contemporary look by mixing bright citrus shades. In this project, several tiles are painted together in a block so that the pattern runs from tile to tile.

MATERIALS

- Off-white glazed ceramic tiles
- Medium and fine paintbrushes
- Non-toxic, water-based, cold-set ceramic paints: dark blue, mid-blue, white and red
- Old saucer

1 Place a block of nine tiles close together. Using a medium paintbrush, paint a blue line down the centre of each tile. Leave to dry.

2 Using a lighter shade of blue, paint a horizontal line across the centre of the tiles. Leave to dry.

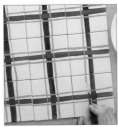

3 Mix a paler blue shade of paint. With a fine brush paint a thin line on each side of the wide vertical and horizontal lines. Leave to dry.

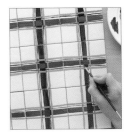

4 Using a very fine paintbrush, paint a thin red line between the blue lines as shown. Leave the tiles to dry thoroughly.

Golden Paisley Tiles

Richly coloured handmade tiles make a perfect base for a motif based on a traditional Moorish design. The tiles are painted freehand so each will be slightly different, adding to their charm. Copy this motif or choose one of a suitable size.

Two different coloured tiles are used here, laid out in a chequerboard pattern with the motif repositioned in alternate squares. You could also position individual paisley tiles to add interest to a wall of plain tiles, or mix other complementary motifs into the scheme.

MATERIALS

- Decorative motif
- Scrap paper
- Pencil
- Scissors
- Handmade coloured ceramic tiles
- Gold non-toxic, water-based, cold-set ceramic paint
- Medium, round paintbrush
- Ceramic tile varnish and brush

1 Copy the motif you have chosen on to paper, adapting it as necessary.

2 Cut several pieces of paper the same size as the tiles. Practise painting the motif freehand to get a feel for the brushstrokes.

3 Paint the motif on to the tile. Leave to dry thoroughly.

4 Seal the surface of the tile with a coat of ceramic tile varnish. Leave to dry thoroughly.

Stamped Star Tiles

Ready-made stamps are widely available in a huge range of designs and you can stamp on to tiles as easily as on to paper or fabric. The technique is simple and quick to do, and will enable you to decorate enough tiles for a wall in very little time. The simple border stripes on some of the tiles are painted with the aid of a stencil.

This dramatic colour scheme complements the purchased dark blue tiles perfectly. You can use any colour tile and choose your own contrasting colours to fit in with your home.

MATERIALS

- Broad, flat paintbrush
- Non-toxic, water-based, cold-set ceramic paints: lime green and blue
- Rubber stamp with star motif
- Plain dark blue glazed ceramic tiles
- Craft knife
- Cutting mat
- Oiled stencil card (cardboard)
- Pencil
- Metal ruler
- Scrap paper
- Protective face mask
- Spray ceramic varnish

1 Using a broad paintbrush, stipple paint on to the rubber stamp. Press the stamp gently on to the centre of the tile. Lift the stamp off carefully, taking care not to smudge the image. Repeat on as many tiles as you need and leave to dry.

2 Using a craft knife and cutting mat, cut a strip of stencil card (cardboard) about 3 cm (1½ in) wide and slightly longer than the tile. Draw a long, thin rectangle about 1 cm (½ in) wide and the length of the tile in the centre of the strip. Cut out the rectangle.

3 Place the stencil on the tile, positioning the border where you want it. Stipple blue paint through the stencil on to the tile. Don't overload the brush, and remove excess paint before each application. Remove the stencil carefully and repeat on the opposite side of the tile. Leave to dry.

4 Working in a well-ventilated area and wearing a face mask, spray with an even coat of ceramic varnish, holding the can about 30 cm (12 in) from the tile. Leave to dry.

Silver Decoupage Tile

This sumptuous and wonderfully decadent tile is not intended for practical use but to be displayed in a box frame or presented as a gift. The surface of the tile is covered with a composite metal leaf, a cheaper alternative to gold and silver leaf, then decorated with a decoupage image photocopied from a book.

For instructions on fixing tiles into a box frame, see the Framed Tile Pictures project.

MATERIALS
- Plain white glazed ceramic tile
- Water-based Italian size and brush
- Aluminium composite loose leaf
- Large, soft brush
- Purple water-based ink
- Paintbrush
- Black-and-white photocopy
- Scissors
- PVA (white) glue
- Ceramic tile varnish and brush

1 Clean the surface of the tile thoroughly to remove any grease (see Basic Techniques). Apply a thin, even coat of size, making sure the whole area is covered. Leave for 15-20 minutes until the size is tacky.

2 Carefully lay the aluminium leaf on to the tile. Use a large, dry, soft brush to burnish the leaf flat and remove any excess.

3 Paint a thin wash of diluted purple ink over the photocopy and leave to dry. Cut out the image. Apply a thin coat of PVA (white) glue to the back and position it on the tile, smoothing the paper gently to remove any air bubbles.

4 Leave the image to dry thoroughly. Seal the surface of the tile with two thin coats of ceramic varnish, allowing about 30 minutes between each coat.

Sea Panel

This cheerful panel is painted freehand across a block of tiles. The paint is applied in several layers, working from light to dark, to give depth and to intensify the colours. A fine coloured outline defines the shapes. This method of tile painting is quite time-consuming so it is perfect for a small panel such as this, or for individual tiles to set among a wall of plain tiles.

MATERIALS
- Plain white glazed ceramic tiles
- Soft pencil
- Non-toxic, water-based, cold-set ceramic paints
- Paintbrushes
- Old saucer

1 Lay the tiles out to make a panel, as close together as possible. Use a soft pencil to sketch your design, leaving room round the panel for the border.

2 Starting with the lightest tones of each colour, paint in the fish, shell and seaweed motifs. Don't paint solid colour, but let patches of the white background show through. Leave to dry.

3 Using mid-tones of each colour, loosely paint darker areas to give depth to the sea motifs.

4 Fill in the background sea with diluted blue paint, applied with a light brushstroke to allow some of the background to show.

5 Using a fine paintbrush and a darker tone of each colour, outline the motifs. Add decorative details as shown.

6 Using a broad brush, paint a border around the panel. Take the paint over the edges of the tiles where they butt up so there are no ugly gaps. Leave to dry.

Rosebud Tiles

These deliciously pretty sugar-pink tiles are sponged in two shades of pale pink, then painted with tiny rosebuds. The sponging technique is very simple and you don't have to use a natural sponge – an ordinary bath sponge works very well provided it has a well-defined, open texture.

The golden rule is to allow the paint to dry thoroughly between coats, otherwise the sponged effect will blur and flatten.

MATERIALS

- Non-toxic, water-based, cold-set ceramic paints: pink, white, red and green
- Old saucer
- Natural sponge or highly textured nylon sponge
- Plain white glazed ceramic tiles
- Medium paintbrush

1 Mix pink paint with white to give a very pale pink. Dip the sponge in the paint and apply randomly over the tile, leaving white spaces here and there. Leave to dry thoroughly.

2 Add more pink to the mixed paint to darken it. Sponge this colour over the tile, allowing the first colour to show through. Leave to dry thoroughly, then sponge a little white paint over the top.

3 Using red paint and a paintbrush, paint rosebud shapes randomly on to the sponged tile – don't make them look too symmetrical.

4 Using green paint, add three leaves to each rosebud as shown. Leave to dry thoroughly.

Mexican Animal Tiles

The rough texture and colour of handmade terracotta tiles makes a perfect background for these naive images based on Mexican designs. Copy the animals and sun shown here or use images from design source books.

Alternate the painted tiles with plain terracotta tiles on a table top or wall, or use a variety of motifs as a continuous border. Terracotta is very porous so you should seal the surface of the tiles with ceramic varnish if they are likely to get damp.

MATERIALS

- Scrap paper
- Metal ruler
- Pencil
- Coloured felt-tip pens
- Tracing paper
- Scissors
- Small unglazed terracotta tiles
- Matt, non-toxic, water-based, cold-set ceramic paints in a variety of colours
- Medium and fine paintbrushes
- Matt varnish or terracotta tile sealant and brush

1 Draw a square the same size as the tile on paper. Trace the designs from the back of the book on to scrap paper and fill them in with coloured pens.

2 When you are satisfied with the designs, lay tracing paper over each drawing and trace the outline and details. Cut out around the outline of each motif to make templates.

3 Position each template in the centre of a tile and draw around it in pencil. Copy the details freehand. Paint the designs, following your original drawings for colour reference. Leave to dry.

4 Using a fine paintbrush, paint a thin black outline around each motif. Leave to dry. Seal the surface of the tiles if necessary, following the manufacturer's instructions.

Sunburst Rose Tiles

Freehand painting gives a liveliness and very attractive spontaneity that can never be achieved with commercially mass-produced tiles. This design is inspired by Mexican folk art and is partly sponged and partly painted. The blue curlicues at the corners add an exuberant note. Mix individual painted tiles with plain white tiles or make a whole wall of sunshine and roses.

MATERIALS

- Non-toxic, water-based, cold-set ceramic paints: orange, yellow, red, green and royal blue
- Old saucer
- Natural sponge or highly textured nylon sponge
- Plain white glazed ceramic tiles
- Medium paintbrush

1 Mix a strong orange-yellow shade of paint. Using a sponge, dab some paint in the centre of the tile to give a mottled sunburst effect. Leave to dry.

2 Using a paintbrush and red paint, loosely paint a rose in the centre of the sunburst. Leave to dry.

3 Using green paint, add two leaves and a short stem. Use the same loose, freehand style as for the rose.

4 Using royal blue ceramic paint, add curlicues at each corner as shown. Leave to dry completely.

Cartoon Tiles

Trace these jolly designs from the back of the book, outline the shapes in a dark colour, then fill them in with jewel-bright shades. The bold designs are ideal for a child's bedroom — use individual tiles or create a frieze round the top of the wall or skirting board (base board). Alternatively, scatter a few tiles among brightly coloured plain tiles for a cheerful bath surround or splashback.

MATERIALS

- Tracing paper
- Pencil
- Plain white glazed ceramic tiles
- Fine paintbrush
- Non-toxic, water-based, cold-set ceramic paints in a variety of colours

1 Trace the motifs from the back of the book, enlarging if necessary to fit the tile (see Basic Techniques). Position the tracing squarely face down on the tile and scribble over the back to transfer the design.

2 Using a fine paintbrush and a strong colour such as dark green, paint over the outlines. Leave to dry. Drawing freehand, add spots to the background area. Allow to dry.

3 Carefully fill in the outlined areas, using bright colours.

4 Finally, fill in the outlined spots and paint spots on the fish. Leave the tiles to dry thoroughly.

Cactus Tiles

Turn your kitchen into a Spanish cantina with these witty tiles! The handmade white tiles have a slightly uneven texture which adds to the rustic effect. The cactus tiles would look good as a panel within a tiled wall, or as spots of colour among plain tiles.

You could paint yellow cacti with a green background or vary the background colours entirely. Solvent-based ceramic paints are used in this project. When you are decorating tiles with this kind of paint, you should always work in a well-ventilated area.

MATERIALS

- Chinagraph pencil (optional)
- Tracing paper (optional)
- Pencil (optional)
- Handmade white glazed ceramic tiles
- Medium and fine paintbrushes
- Non-toxic, solvent-based, cold-set ceramic paints: light green, mid-green and golden yellow
- Old saucer
- Varnish, as recommended by the paint manufacturer, and brush

1 Using a chinagraph pencil, draw the outline of a cactus on the tile. Alternatively, enlarge the template from the back of the book and transfer to the tile (see Basic Techniques).

2 Using a medium paintbrush, fill in the cactus shape with light green paint. Leave to dry.

3 Using a fine paintbrush and mid-green paint, outline the cactus, then add ridges and spines as shown.

4 Starting in the middle of the tile, fill in the background with golden yellow paint, leaving a white outline around the cactus to accentuate it. Leave to dry, then seal with varnish.

Sgraffito Fish Tiles

Two shades of blue create a serene atmosphere. The details are incised into the wet paint in a traditional form of decoration known as sgraffito. If you are making a set of tiles, paint them one at a time so that the paint does not dry before you add the sgraffito.

MATERIALS

- Chinagraph pencil (optional)
- Tracing paper (optional)
- Pencil (optional)
- Plain white glazed ceramic tiles
- Non-toxic, solvent-based, cold-set ceramic paints: dark blue and turquoise blue
- Medium paintbrushes
- Old saucer
- Engraver's scribing tool or sharp pencil
- Varnish, as recommended by the paint manufacturer, and brush

1 Using a chinagraph pencil, draw the outline of the fish on to the tile. Alternatively, enlarge the template from the back of the book and transfer to the tile (see Basic Techniques).

2 Fill in the fish shape with dark blue paint using a medium paintbrush.

3 While the paint is still wet, scratch decorative details on to the fish shape with an engraver's scribing tool or sharp pencil.

4 Fill in the background with turquoise blue, leaving a fine white outline around the fish. Scratch a swirl at each corner as shown. Leave to dry completely, then seal the surface with a coat of varnish.

Daisy Tiles

Make it summer all year round with these fresh-as-a-daisy tiles! They would make a wonderful border to a wall of plain white tiles, or add individual spots of interest. You can vary the dark blue background colour to suit your own colour scheme — a pale blue or scarlet background would completely alter the effect. Remember that solvent-based ceramic paints should only be used in a well-ventilated area.

MATERIALS

- Chinagraph pencil (optional)
- Tracing paper (optional)
- Pencil (optional)
- Plain white glazed ceramic tiles
- Non-toxic, solvent-based, cold-set ceramic paints: yellow, green, warm grey and dark blue
- Old saucer
- Medium paintbrush
- Varnish, as recommended by the paint manufacturer, and brush

1 Using a chinagraph pencil, draw a daisy flower and leaves on the tile. Alternatively, enlarge the template from the back of the book and transfer to the tile (see Basic Techniques).

2 Paint the flower centre yellow. Mix some green paint into the yellow to make light green, then fill in the leaves. Leave to dry.

3 Add veins to the leaves with dark green paint. Add a darker yellow shadow to the flower centre, to give it depth. Outline one edge of each petal with warm grey paint. Leave to dry.

4 Fill in the background with dark blue paint. Start in the centre, painting up to the edges of the daisy, and work outwards. Leave to dry thoroughly, then seal the surface with varnish.

Medieval Floor Tiles

Small, shaped tiles were used to decorate the tessellated floors of medieval churches with geometric patterns. This type of decorative tiling was revived by the Victorians to create patterns on paths, doorsteps and hallways.

Here, whole terracotta tiles are cleverly painted to create the same effect. Butt them together to make a large repeating design. Ceramic paints are quite durable, but do not place the tiles in areas of heavy traffic or outdoors.

MATERIALS

- Unglazed terracotta tiles
- Ceramic sealant and brush
- Metal ruler
- Pencil
- Non-toxic, water-based, cold-set ceramic paints in a variety of colours
- Old saucer
- Medium paintbrushes
- Rubber stamp with star motif

1 Seal the porous surface of the tile with a coat of ceramic sealant. Leave to dry.

2 Draw the geometric design on the tile as shown, using a ruler and pencil.

3 Paint the design, using rich medieval-style colours. Leave to dry thoroughly.

4 Using a paintbrush, apply an even coating of paint to the rubber stamp, then press it down firmly on to the centre of the tile. Leave to dry completely.

American Folk Art Tiles

These simple, homey motifs were very popular with early American settlers such as the Amish and the Pennsylvania Dutch. They reappear on many household items, including wooden blanket chests, patchwork quilts and punched tinware.

The tiles are first painted with emulsion (latex) paint before being stencilled with the design. They are sealed with several coats of acrylic varnish so are tough enough to lay as a floor covering.

MATERIALS

- Unglazed terracotta tiles
- Emulsion (latex) paint: two pale colours and three dark colours
- Large paintbrushes
- Scissors
- Oiled stencil card (cardboard)
- Tracing paper
- Pencil
- Craft knife
- Cutting mat
- Old saucer
- Natural sponge
- Cottonwool buds
- Water-based acrylic varnish and brush

1 Paint each tile with two coats of pale-coloured emulsion (latex) paint. The colours will make a pleasing contrast when the tiles are placed together.

2 Cut a piece of stencil card (cardboard) for each motif. Trace the motifs from the back of the book. Transfer one on to the centre of each piece of card (see Basic Techniques). Using a craft knife and cutting mat, cut out each motif.

3 Pour a little dark-coloured emulsion paint into a saucer. Place each stencil on a tile, then sponge the paint through the stencils on to the tiles.

4 Using a different colour of dark emulsion and a cottonwool bud, decorate the top and bottom of some tiles with a row of dots. Leave to dry.

5 Seal the tiles with at least four coats of varnish, allowing each coat to dry thoroughly before applying the next.

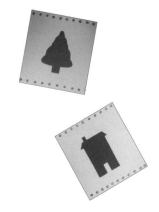

Foam Stamp Tiles

Ready-made rubber stamps are very popular but it is cheaper and much more fun to make your own from foam rubber, available from specialist shops. Foam is very smooth and dense so it gives a clear, crisp image. The bold, bright colours give a very modern feel.

MATERIALS

- Scissors
- High-density foam rubber
- Tracing paper
- Pencil
- Fine marker pen
- Cutting mat
- Craft knife
- Masking tape
- Unglazed terracotta
- small inset tiles
- Non-toxic, water-based, cold-set ceramic paints in a variety of colours
- Old saucer
- Natural sponge
- Medium paintbrush

1 Cut a piece of foam 7 cm (2¾ in) square for each stamp. Trace and transfer the templates from the back of the book to the foam. Place the foam on a cutting mat and cut round the shape, using a craft knife. Remove only half the depth of foam.

2 Cut strips of masking tape and lay them as a thin border around the edges of the tiles.

3 Pour some ceramic paint into a saucer. Using a sponge, spread it over the surface of the tile. You will probably need to apply more than one coat to give a dense, even colour. Allow each coat to dry completely before applying the next.

4 Using a paintbrush, apply an even coating of paint to a foam stamp, then press it down firmly on to the centre of a tile. Repeat with the other tiles and leave to dry.

Seaside Tiles

These bright and breezy tiles with their seaside-inspired motifs would look great in a kitchen, bathroom or even a beach hut. The charming, naive designs evoke memories of salty air, sand between the toes and the gentle art of rock-pool gazing.

The raised design is squeezed on to the tile rather like toothpaste, in a decorative process called tube-lining, which was very popular around the turn of the century. The areas bordered by the lines are then filled in with ceramic paint to complete the design.

MATERIALS

- Tracing paper
- Pencil
- Carbon paper
- Plain white glazed ceramic tiles
- Tube of non-toxic, water-based black outline paint
- Medium paintbrushes
- Non-toxic water-based cold set ceramic paints
- Old saucer

1 Trace the designs from the back of the book, enlarging to fit your tile. Place a piece of carbon paper face-down on the tile. Lay the tracing on top. Redraw over the lines to transfer the design.

2 Draw over the designs using the black outline paint. If the line breaks, simply move back and repair it. Leave the tile to dry, following the manufacturer's instructions.

3 When the outlines are dry, fill in the designs using the water-based ceramic paints. You may have to apply two coats to get a good, opaque finish.

4 Add decorative details, such as dots, freehand, and leave the paint to dry thoroughly, following the manufacturer's instructions.

Art Deco Tiles

The strong colours and clean geometric lines of **Art Deco** are ideal for decorative tiles. This design is adapted from a textile pattern of 1924 and shows how you can find inspiration for tiles in many different sources. The asymmetrical design means that the tiles can be arranged in a variety of combinations to give different repeat designs. You may wish to sketch the design on paper to experiment with different patterns.

MATERIALS

- Pencil
- Metal ruler
- Plain white glazed ceramic tiles
- Non-toxic acrylic paints: black, green and yellow
- Old saucer
- Fine and medium paintbrushes
- Water-based acrylic varnish and brush

1 Using a pencil and ruler, copy the geometric design from the back of the book on to the tile. Fill in the black areas of the design with paint, keeping the edges crisp and neat. Leave to dry.

2 Fill in the green and yellow areas of the design. You may need to apply more than one coat to get a flat, solid colour.

3 Finally add decorative green lines, making them as straight as possible. Leave to dry completely, then seal the surface of the tiles with two coats of varnish, allowing it to dry between coats.

Art Nouveau Tiles

These highly stylized designs are inspired by the work of Charles Rennie Mackintosh and the Glasgow School at the turn of the century. The rose and thorned-stem tiles can be used together in blocks or as a border. Try reversing the stem stencil on some of the tiles. Repositionable spray adhesive was used for this project and is very useful for holding the stencil in place while you apply paint to each tile. Oiled stencil card (cardboard) is fairly hard-wearing and will last long enough to enable you to stencil many tiles.

MATERIALS
- Tracing paper
- Pencil
- Plain white glazed ceramic tiles
- Scissors
- Oiled stencil card (cardboard)
- Craft knife
- Cutting mat
- Protective face mask
- Repositionable spray adhesive
- Large and fine paintbrushes
- Non-toxic acrylic paints: light green, dark green, deep red and white
- Old saucer
- Water-based acrylic varnish and brush

1 Trace the rose and stem designs from the back of the book to fit your tiles. Cut two pieces of stencil card the same size as the tiles and transfer one design to each (see Basic Techniques). Using a craft knife and a cutting mat, cut away the centre of each design.

2 Wearing a protective face mask, lightly spray the back of the stencils with adhesive. Place the stem stencil on a tile. Using a dry brush, apply light green paint to the leaves and dark green for the stalk. Leave to dry.

3 Add a little deep red paint to pick out the thorns on the stem.

4 Mix deep red paint with white to make a dusky pink. Stencil the rose motif on to another tile. Leave to dry.

5 Add a little deep red paint around the edges of the petals to emphasize the shape of the rose and give it depth.

6 Using a fine paintbrush, add a few light green dots in the centre of the rose. Leave to dry, then seal the surface of the tiles with two coats of varnish, allowing them to dry between coats.

Heraldic Dragon Tiles

1 Trace the dragon design from the back of the book, enlarging it if necessary, and transfer on to the tile using a ballpoint pen (see Basic Techniques).

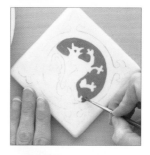

2 Lighten the terracotta by adding a little white paint. Carefully fill in the background to the dragon motif.

3 Add more terracotta paint to darken the colour slightly, then fill in the outer background edges of the tile. Leave to dry completely.

4 Seal the surface of the tile with two coats of matt acrylic varnish, allowing it to dry between coats.

This appealing dragon is based on a tile on the floor of a medieval cathedral. Mythical and heraldic motifs such as this are combined in the floor with geometric tiles to make a vivid, overall design.

Many of these medieval tiles were made by the encaustic technique, stamped with a design which was then filled with clay in a contrasting colour. This project uses two shades of terracotta paint to recreate the design but these tiles are not suitable for use as floor tiles.

MATERIALS

- Tracing paper
- Pencil
- Dark cream glazed ceramic tiles
- Ballpoint pen
- Non-toxic acrylic paints: terracotta and white
- Old saucer
- Fine paintbrushes
- Matt acrylic varnish and brush

Persian Carnation Tiles

In the 15th century magnificent tile friezes were an important element in **Ottoman Turkish** architecture. The palace of **Suleyman the Magnificent** in Istanbul contains stunning examples of these friezes. Stylized flower designs were popular, especially carnations and tulips. These tiles make an intricate interlocking pattern, which would look beautiful used as an all-over decoration.

MATERIALS

- Tracing paper
- Pencil
- Plain white glazed ceramic tiles
- Non-toxic acrylic paints: light pink, dark pink, light blue, dark blue, light green, dark green and lemon yellow
- Old saucer
- Fine paintbrushes
- Water-based acrylic varnish and brush

1 Trace the carnation design from the back of the book, enlarging it if necessary, and transfer on to the tile (see Basic Techniques). Paint the flowers in the centre and corners light pink. Leave to dry, then emphasize the petals with darker pink.

2 Add light blue petals, leave to dry, then emphasize the petals with darker blue paint. Paint the stems and leaves light green.

3 Emphasize the stems and leaves with darker green paint. Fill in the flower centres and corners of the leaves with lemon yellow paint.

4 Paint the small half-flowers with light pink and light blue paint. Leave to dry, then emphasize with darker pink paint. When completely dry, seal the surface with two coats of varnish.

Majolica Tiles

This delightful vase of flowers is based on a tile design from the Urbino area of Northern Italy, where the majolica style of pottery decoration developed in the 15th century. The Renaissance-style designs included scrolls, biblical scenes, portraits and plant motifs.

Originally, metal oxides painted on a thick white tin glaze produced vivid colours such as purples, blues, yellows and greens when fired. You can reproduce these bright Mediterranean colours using acrylic paints on plain white tiles.

MATERIALS

- Tracing paper
- Pencil
- Plain white glazed ceramic tiles
- Non-toxic acrylic paints: yellow, light green, dark green, white, orange and royal blue
- Old saucer
- Fine paintbrushes
- Water-based acrylic varnish and brush

1 Trace the vase of flowers design from the back of the book, enlarging it if necessary, and transfer on to the tile (see Basic Techniques). Begin to paint the design with a fine paintbrush, starting with the palest tones of each colour.

2 Carefully paint in the foliage with light and dark green paint leaving each colour to dry before applying the next.

3 Add white to orange paint to create a paler shade. Use to paint the top and bottom of the vase pale orange. Using darker orange, fill in the flower centres and emphasize the shape of the vase.

4 Using royal blue paint, outline the shapes of the flowers and vase. Add the vase handles and decorative details to the flower heads. Leave the tile to dry, then seal the surface with two coats of varnish, allowing it to dry between coats.

Medieval Tiles

This formal, symmetrical design was inspired by the stained glass in Chartres Cathedral, showing once again how you can successfully adapt a design from one medium to another. Paint the black outlines slightly irregularly to look like the divisions in a stained glass window.

The thick, matt-glazed tiles are sealed with matt acrylic varnish. This gives them a smooth, marble-like finish which is very pleasing.

MATERIALS

- Tracing paper
- Handmade white, matt-glazed ceramic tiles
- Non-toxic acrylic paints: grey, pale yellow, red-brown and black
- Old saucer
- Fine and medium paintbrushes
- Matt, water-based acrylic varnish and brush

1 Trace the design from the back of the book, enlarging it if necessary, and transfer on to the tile (see Basic Techniques). Using grey paint and a fine paintbrush, fill in the flower shape in the centre.

2 Using a medium paintbrush, continue to fill in the design, leaving a white outline around the flower. Use pale yellow paint for the diamonds and warm red-brown for the background.

3 Pick out the design details in black paint, using a fine paintbrush. Vary the width of the outlines to imitate stained glass. Leave to dry completely, then seal the surface with two coats of varnish, allowing it to dry between coats.

William Morris Tiles

This gorgeous set of tiles is based on a design by William Morris in 1870. The flowing lines of the flower painting are typical of his bold, naturalistic style and can also be seen on his fabrics and wallpaper designs. Morris's tiles were often manufactured by the famous tile designer William De Morgan, using the lustrous colours for which he is renowned.

MATERIALS
- Tracing paper
- Pencil
- Four plain white glazed ceramic tiles
- Scissors
- Ballpoint pen
- Non-toxic, water-based, cold-set ceramic paints: blue, dark green and white
- Old saucer
- Medium and fine paintbrushes

1 Enlarge the design from the back of the book so that each square fits on to one tile. Cut into four separate patterns. Transfer each pattern on to a tile, drawing over the lines with a ballpoint pen (see Basic Techniques).

2 Dilute some blue paint, then fill in the two main flower shapes with a medium paintbrush. Leave to dry.

3 Using undiluted blue paint and a fine paintbrush, add definition to the petals.

4 Using a medium paintbrush, fill in the leaves with dark green paint. The slightly streaky effect left by the bristles will add movement to the design. Leave the paint to dry completely.

5 Highlight the leaves with white veins.

6 Paint green leaves on the flower tiles. Leave to dry, then highlight with white veins as before. Add detailing and fine outlines to the flowers. Leave the tiles to dry completely.

Byzantine Bird Tile

Translucent paints give this exotic tile the rich, glowing colours identified with **Byzantine** art.

The bird motif is taken from a cloisonné enamel panel originally decorated with precious stones. To suggest this effect, outline the design with a gold pen.

MATERIALS

- Tracing paper
- Pencil
- Plain white glazed ceramic tile
- Non-toxic, water-based, translucent, cold-set ceramic paints in a variety of rich colours
- Old saucer
- Fine paintbrushes
- Gold felt-tip pen

1 Trace the bird design from the back of the book, enlarging it if necessary, and transfer on to the tile (see Basic Techniques). Paint the bird's head and legs, then start to paint the feathers, using several bright colours.

2 Paint the plants, using the colours shown. Leave to dry completely.

3 Using a gold pen, outline every part of the design. Add decorative gold details to the bird's feathers and the plants.

Fruit and Leaf Tiles

These vibrant, loosely painted tiles are ideal for kitchens and could be used to make a panel, a border or add spots of colour in a wall of plain tiles. They have a rustic charm that would enhance a traditional setting, with stripped floorboards or earthenware floor tiles, hand-thrown pottery and country furniture. All the designs are sketched on to the tiles, then painted freehand. If you don't feel confident enough to get it right the first time, practise on a scrap of paper to get a feeling for making long, flowing brush strokes.

MATERIALS

- Soft pencil
- Plain white glazed ceramic tiles
- Medium and fine paintbrushes
- Water-based, non-toxic, glossy acrylic enamel paints in a variety of colours
- Old saucer

1 Using a soft pencil, lightly sketch in the leaf design, making it large enough to fit into the area of the tile comfortably.

2 Using a medium brush, paint a broad, flowing outline around the leaf design, adding a central vein.

3 Paint in the background using broad, loose brushstrokes. Try not to repaint over any area once you have covered it, to avoid making ridges in the surface.

4 Using a fine brush, add details such as the smaller veins in the centre of the leaf. Leave the tile to dry, following the paint manufacturer's instructions.

Pueblan Tiles

The tile-making centre of **Puebla** in Mexico has been famous for vibrant, colourful designs since the 17th century. The mixture of Moorish, Spanish and native Indian cultures has resulted in a huge variety of designs, including highly ornate patterns such as this.

The tiles fit together to form a repeat design, but you can also use them individually in a border with plain coloured tiles. If you plan to use the tiles to create a repeat pattern, ensure the patterns at the edges will match up on each tile.

MATERIALS

- Pencil
- Metal ruler
- Plain white glazed ceramic tiles
- Non-toxic, water-based, cold-set ceramic paints: orange, yellow, royal blue and turquoise
- Old saucer
- Medium paintbrushes

1 Using a pencil and ruler, lightly draw a narrow border around the edge of the tile. Draw a square in each corner. Paint the borders orange and the squares yellow.

2 Using the same colours, paint a design in the centre of the tile as shown. Leave to dry completely.

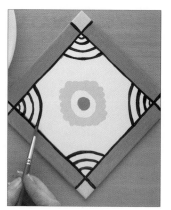

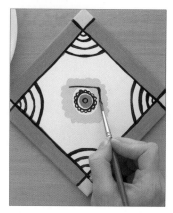

3 Outline the borders and squares in royal blue paint. Then paint blue arcs at each corner as shown.

4 Decorate the centre design with blue paint as shown.

5 Using orange paint, paint a quarter-circle in each corner of the tile to form the repeat. Finally, fill in the background with turquoise paint. Leave to dry.

USING TILES CREATIVELY

The fabulous tile-clad buildings of Antoni Gaudi in Barcelona illustrate the possibilities of working with tiles. Some of his ideas for the broken tile mosaics displayed in the city's gardens were probably inspired by folk art; in India artists have created sculptures covered in mosaic situated in amazing gardens. Mosaic is an ideal method of recycling pieces of ceramic tile to cover surfaces cheaply and durably. With tile mosaic mix bright patterns and textures for impact or collect shades of one colour for a more subtle effect. You can include small whole tiles or mosaic tesserae, and tile shops will often sell broken tiles cheaply.

Design Gallery

Left: *A wonderful, sparkling tiled lizard from the Parc Güell in Barcelona. Created by Antoni Gaudí 1900-1914, the park is decorated with an incredible assortment of tile mosaic sculptures such as this one.*

Below: *Latin countries are famous for their use of tiles. Here at the Plaza Venticimo de Julio in Tenerife, all the seats are lavishly clad with wonderfully decorative tile panels.*

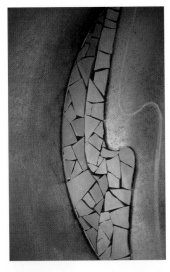

Left: *An abstract pattern is given depth and a three dimensional feel with contrasting colours.*

Far Left: *A luminous table top, covered with a variety of hand-cut tiles, in an elegantly classic design.*

Below left: *A beautifully tiled pool is given a striking border of painted tiles around the edge.*

Below: *A lit cascade water feature in a garden is tiled with small blue tiles for a dramatic effect.*

Above: *Shards of blue and white china are recycled here into a vibrant splashback for a bathroom sink.*

Right: *A design classic reminiscent of Mediterranean cafés, the mosaic table takes many forms. Here, glass tesserae in shades of blue, green and earthy brown make a very cool-looking garden table.*

Left: *Fresh blue and white tiles are used to cover this storage box, making it a perfect decorative addition to a bathroom,*

Right: *A bold triptych of mosaic panels is lavishly decorated with fragments of richly coloured tile. The inventive use of pattern, colour and texture makes it particularly striking.*

Marble and Mosaic Table

Perfect for use in the garden or patio on a hot summer's day, this striking table has a centre of cool marble tiles surrounded by a shimmering blue and gold border. The tumbled marble tiles have a soft, powdery surface that is very smooth to the touch and creates a pleasing contrast to the hard glass mosaic tesserae.

The table top is made separately and then set into a wooden frame. Alternatively, you could use a commercially bought pine table with a detachable top. It is a good idea to seal the marble tiles, otherwise they may stain; the mosaic tesserae do not need sealing. Of course, you can substitute different colourways according to preference.

MATERIALS

- Large sheet of scrap paper slightly larger than the table top
- Pencil
- Metal ruler
- White tumbled marble tiles
- Glass mosaic tesserae: blue and gold
- Protective leather gloves
- Safety goggles
- Mosaic nippers
- PVA (white) glue and brush
- Protective face mask
- Handsaw
- 12 mm ($^9/_{16}$ in) waterproof plywood
- Craft knife
- Rubber gloves
- All-in-one flexible waterproof tile adhesive and grout
- Notched spreader
- Household paintbrush
- Foam scouring pad
- Sponge
- Lint-free cloth
- Marble tile sealant and brush (optional)

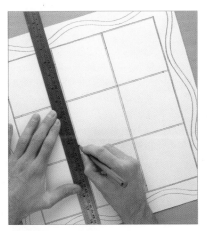

1 Draw a plan of your table top on paper and mark out the design, remembering to allow space between the tiles for grouting. Draw a wavy line along the border as shown.

2 Roughly lay out the marble tiles and glass tesserae on the paper plan to estimate the number of tiles you will need.

3 Wearing protective gloves and goggles, cut the gold tesserae to size with mosaic nippers. Clear away any shards of glass immediately and dispose of them carefully.

4 Spread a little PVA (white) glue on the front of each piece of tessera. Stick them face down on the paper plan, following the wavy line.

5 Cut the blue mosaic tesserae in the same way. (Even if there is room for whole tesserae, cut ones will look better.) Glue them to the paper plan either side of the gold wavy line.

6 Wearing a face mask, cut a piece of plywood 2 mm ($\frac{1}{16}$ in) larger all round than the paper plan. Seal both sides with PVA (white) glue and leave to dry. Key (scuff) the surface with a craft knife.

7 Place the paper plan face up on a cutting mat. Using a craft knife, carefully cut away the paper from the centre of the design to leave the mosaic border.

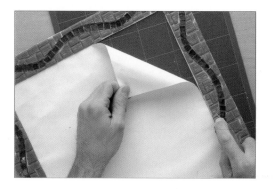

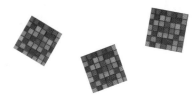

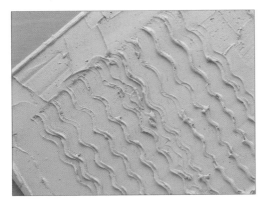

8 Wearing rubber gloves, spread a thick layer of tile adhesive over the plywood. Use the grooved side of the spreader to key the surface for the tiles to adhere to.

9 Carefully lower the mosaic face-down on to the tile adhesive so that the tiles at the edges do not fall off. Smooth extra adhesive around the outside of the border to cover the cut edges of the tiles.

10 Position the marble tiles and press them into the tile adhesive. Leave to dry for 24 hours.

11 Using a paintbrush and water, soak the paper. Leave for 15 minutes, then peel it off the mosaic. Use a foam scouring pad to remove any stubborn traces of paper and glue. Leave to dry.

12 Grout the whole table top, removing extra grout with a damp sponge. Polish the surface with a dry, lint-free cloth. Seal the marble tiles if desired.

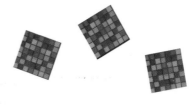

Mosaic Bedhead

The daisy-filled panels of this pine bedhead would look beautiful in a country bedroom with distressed wooden furniture. Make a footboard to match or use the same design to decorate other panelled furniture, such as a kitchen unit or an interior door. Mosaic is very heavy so make sure the furniture joints and any hinges and the floor can carry the extra weight. **Admix is a compound used with the tile adhesive to make it more flexible.**

Instead of folk art flowers, consider other themes for different areas of the house: for a bed in a child's room for example, a design such as snakes and ladders would work well.

MATERIALS

- Unvarnished pine bedhead and footboard
- PVA (white) glue and brush
- Craft knife
- Old palette knife or flexible spreader
- Cement-based tile adhesive and admix
- Soft pencil
- Protective leather gloves
- Safety goggles
- Piece of heavy sacking
- Hammer
- Plain glazed ceramic tiles: white, orange, green and honey-coloured
- Mosaic nippers
- Rubber gloves
- Rubber-edged spreader
- Lint-free cloth
- Sponge
- Protective face mask
- Sanding block

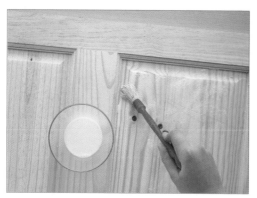

1 Seal the surface of the wood with PVA (white) glue.

2 Score the surface of the wood with a craft knife.

3 Using a palette knife or flexible spreader, fill any recesses in the areas to be decorated with tile adhesive. Leave for 24 hours to allow the adhesive to set.

4 Draw a daisy design on the panels with a soft pencil.

5 Wearing protective leather gloves and goggles, wrap each white and orange tile separately in sacking and break them with a hammer (see Basic Techniques). Trim the white tile pieces into petal shapes with mosaic nippers. Trim the orange tile pieces into round centres for the daisies.

6 Wearing rubber gloves, spread tile adhesive over the daisy shapes on the panels. Press the white and orange mosaic pieces in place to make flowers.

7 Wearing protective clothing, smash the green tiles as before. Shape the pieces with tile nippers to make stems and leaves.

8 Spread tile adhesive over the appropriate areas of the design, then press the green mosaic pieces into position to make leaves and stems. Leave to dry for 24 hours.

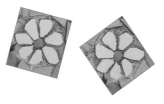

9 Wearing protective clothing, smash the honey-coloured tiles as before. Spread tile adhesive around the daisies and fill in the background, cutting the pieces of tile as necessary to fit.

10 Wearing rubber gloves and using a rubber-edged spreader or lint-free cloth, spread more adhesive over the mosaic. Push the adhesive well down into the spaces and make sure that all sharp corners are covered. Remove excess adhesive with a damp sponge, then leave to dry for 24 hours.

11 Wearing a face mask, lightly smooth the surface of the mosaic with a sanding block. Polish with a dry, lint-free cloth.

Door Number Plaque

A mosaic door plaque adds a distinctive personal touch and will withstand all weathers. Plan the design carefully so that you have space between the numbers and the border to fit neatly cut tesserae. The "indirect" method of mosaic is very convenient. It was originally devised to allow mosaic-makers to create their designs away from the site intended for the finished piece. The tesserae are glued face-down onto paper and then applied to another surface when the design is complete. When using this method, you can work at your own pace without worrying that the adhesive will set before you have finished.

MATERIALS

- Scissors
- Craft paper
- Pencil
- Metal ruler
- Floor tile
- Mosaic tesserae:
  turquoise, black
  and yellow
- PVA (white) glue and brush
- Protective leather gloves
- Safety goggles
- Mosaic nippers
- Protective face mask
- Rubber gloves
- Cement-based
  powdered grout
- Notched spreader
- Sponge
- Flexible, waterproof,
  cement-based tile
  adhesive
- Lint-free cloth

1 Cut a piece of craft paper the same size as the tile. Mark the border and number in reverse on the shiny side of the paper. The border is one tessera wide. There should be room between the border and numbers to insert a quarter-tessera neatly.

2 Dilute the PVA (white) glue 50/50 with water. Glue the flat sides of the turquoise tesserae on to the paper border, with a black tessera at each corner.

3 Wearing protective leather gloves and goggles, cut some black tesserae with mosaic nippers to make rectangles. Glue the black rectangles flat-side down over the paper numbers.

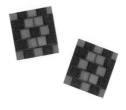

4 Wearing protective leather gloves and goggles, cut yellow tesserae into quarter-squares. Lay them around the straight edges of the numerals, using the nippers to cut to size as necessary. Glue them flat side down as before. Place quarter-square tesserae around curved edges, cutting as necessary.

5 Wearing a face mask, goggles and rubber gloves, mix the grout according to the manufacturer's instructions. Grout the finished mosaic with the spreader, removing the excess with a damp sponge. Leave to dry. Spread a layer of tile adhesive over the floor tile and key (scuff) with the notched edge of the spreader.

6 Put the grouted mosaic paper-side down on a flat surface. Place the floor tile on top, matching corners and edges. Press the tile down, wipe away excess adhesive and leave to dry.

7 Using a sponge and water, soak the paper on the front of the mosaic. Leave for 15 minutes.

8 Lift one corner of the paper to see if it comes away cleanly. If it does, peel the paper off, otherwise leave it to soak a little longer.

9 Wipe away any surplus glue. Wearing rubber gloves, re-grout the plaque, including the sides. Remove excess grout with a damp sponge, then polish the surface with a dry, lint-free cloth.

Crazy Paving Shelf

Transform your kitchen with a three-dimensional mosaic worthy of the great Gaudí himself! The top of this shelf is exuberantly decorated in random colours, reminiscent of Gaudí's garden mosaics in Barcelona. You can also achieve a quite different effect by using shades of one colour.

If you are using tiles of different thickness, apply a generous layer of tile adhesive to give them a firm base. The mosaic will make the shelf quite heavy, so make sure it is attached firmly to the wall with the appropriate fixings.

If you are using the shelf in a kitchen, why not consider tiling a work surface in whole tiles using the same colours, or continue the crazy paving pattern on kitchen cabinets.

MATERIALS

- Tape measure
- Ready-made wooden shelf, with brackets
- Protective face mask
- Saw
- 1.5 cm (¾ in) MDF (medium-density fibreboard) or pine
- Metal cuphooks
- Pencil
- Workbench and clamps
- Drill
- Wood glue
- Screwdriver and screws
- Protective leather gloves
- Safety goggles
- Assorted plain glazed ceramic tiles
- Piece of heavy sacking
- Hammer
- Mosaic nippers
- Flexible tile adhesive
- Notched spreader
- Rubber gloves
- Grout colourant
- Powdered grout
- Face mask
- Sponge
- Lint-free cloth

1 Measure the distance between the shelf brackets. Wearing a face mask, cut a backing strip of MDF (medium-density fibreboard) or pine to fit.

2 Space the cuphooks at equal distances on the backing strip and draw round them. Clamp the backing strip, then drill the screw holes. Drill a hole at either end as extra fixing.

3 Mark the position of the backing strip between the shelf brackets. Using clamps, drill a hole in each bracket, then drill a hole at either end of the backing strip to match. Glue the backing strip in place, then screw firmly together.

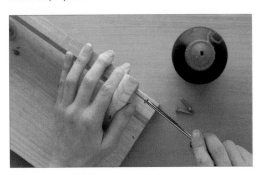

4 Wearing protective leather gloves and goggles, wrap each tile separately in sacking and break with a hammer (see Basic Techniques). Trim the pieces into triangles with mosaic nippers.

5 Spread a thick layer of tile adhesive over one-third of the shelf top. Using the notched edge of the spreader, key (scuff) the surface, then press pieces of multicoloured tile into the adhesive.

6 Cut square and rectangular pieces from the original edges of the blue tiles. Remove any sharp pieces. Apply the tile pieces to the shelf edges as before, to give them a smooth, safe finish. Complete the rest of the shelf top.

7 Apply adhesive to the backing strip as before, leaving spaces for the cuphooks. Break the blue tiles and cut into triangles as before, then cover the backing strip and brackets with blue mosaic. Leave the shelf to dry thoroughly.

8 Wearing rubber gloves, goggles and a face mask, mix dry grout colourant into the dry grout powder, following the manufacturer's instructions. Add water and mix thoroughly (see Basic Techniques).

9 Spread the grout over the shelf, pushing it well down into the spaces between the pieces of tile and making sure that any sharp edges are covered. Remove excess grout with a damp sponge. Leave to dry completely, then polish the surface with a dry, lint-free cloth.

Tiled Tray

Tile mosaic need not always be random and multicoloured. In this elegant design, the intense blue border is made from whole tiles and the centre panel is covered with crazy mosaic but in plain white. For a completely different effect, use brightly-coloured tiles for the mosaic and contain the design with a formal border in a plain dark colour or black.

Ensure the tiles you use for the tray are of the same thickness, so that you can create a flat surface. The tiles should have a satin- or matt-glazed finish instead of highly glazed ones, which would be too slippery for practical use.

MATERIALS

- Unvarnished pine tray
- PVA (white) glue and brush
- Craft knife
- Blue matt-glazed ceramic border tiles
- Set square (T-square)
- Pencil
- Large scissors (optional)
- Protective leather gloves
- Safety goggles
- Plain white matt-glazed ceramic tiles
- Piece of heavy sacking
- Hammer
- Rubber gloves
- Notched spreader
- Flexible, cement-based tile adhesive
- Sponge
- Protective face mask
- Sanding block

1 Seal all surfaces of the tray with diluted PVA (white) glue. When the wood is dry, key (scuff) the surface with a craft knife.

2 Lay out the blue border tiles around the inside edge of the tray to work out where the border should fall. If the tiles do not fit exactly, move the border in and leave a narrow space around the outside to fill in with mosaic. Mark the border position with a set square (T-square).

3 If necessary, cut the border tiles into strips. Wearing protective leather gloves and goggles, wrap each white tile separately in sacking and break with a hammer (see Basic Techniques).

4 Wearing rubber gloves and using the notched edge of a spreader, apply a layer of tile adhesive over the marked border area. Set the border tiles in position. Apply more adhesive to the outside edge and fit in pieces of white mosaic. Fill in the centre panel. Leave to dry.

5 Wearing rubber gloves, spread more tile adhesive over the surface of the mosaic, making sure that any sharp edges are covered. Press uneven pieces down firmly, and press the adhesive down among the pieces. Remove excess adhesive with a damp sponge.

6 Leave the tray to dry for 24 hours. Wearing a face mask, use a sanding block to remove any remaining adhesive.

Boat Splashback

A detachable mosaic splashback makes a very practical surface above a bathroom sink, being strong and durable as well as waterproof. This jaunty boat design is made entirely from broken tile mosaic – sort the pieces into groups of each colour to make it easier when you are working on the picture.

Flashes of mirror tile give the splashback an extra sparkling quality.

MATERIALS

- 1 cm (½ in) plywood, cut to the desired size
- PVA (white) glue and brush
- Craft knife
- Pencil
- Work bench and clamps
- Bradawl
- Protective leather gloves
- Safety goggles
- Plain glazed ceramic tiles: red, pale blue, dark blue and white
- Mirror tiles
- Piece of heavy sacking
- Hammer
- Mosaic nippers
- Rubber gloves
- Old knife or flexible spreader
- Flexible, waterproof cement-based tile adhesive
- White glazed ceramic tile border strip
- Sponge
- Scissors
- Plastic drinking straw
- Protective face mask
- Sanding block
- Lint-free cloth
- Yacht varnish and brush

1 Seal the front and back of the plywood with diluted PVA (white) glue. Leave to dry, then score the front of the board with a craft knife.

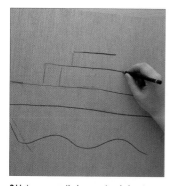

2 Using a pencil, draw a simple boat design on the front of the board. Place the board on a work bench, then clamp in position. Use a bradawl to make a screw hole in each corner.

3 Wearing protective leather gloves and goggles, wrap each tile separately in sacking and break with a hammer (see Basic Techniques). Trim the pieces with mosaic nippers if necessary. Wearing rubber gloves and using a knife or flexible spreader, spread tile adhesive within the lines of the drawing. Build up the shape, leaving the portholes and windows blank.

4 Fill in the background sea and sky with light blue tile pieces. Continue to within 1 cm ($\frac{1}{2}$ in) of the edge of the board, avoiding the screw holes.

5 Wearing protective leather gloves and goggles, cut the white border strip into short lengths with mosaic nippers. Fill in the border around the edges of the design, working as before. Leave a gap between each border piece for grouting.

6 Add pieces of mirror tile to make the portholes and windows. Remove excess adhesive from the surface of the splashback with a damp sponge. Leave to dry for 24 hours. Push a length of drinking straw into each hole.

7 Wearing rubber gloves, spread more tile adhesive over the surface, covering any sharp edges. Smooth the adhesive around the straws. Remove excess adhesive with a damp sponge, then leave the splashback to dry for 24 hours. Wearing a face mask, smooth the surface lightly with a sanding block, then polish with a dry, lint-free cloth. Seal the back of the board with two coats of yacht varnish, drying between coats.

Tiled Mirror Frame

This sophisticated design is composed of small floor tile insets edged with strips of mirror tile. The colours and simple geometric shapes give it a strong **Art Deco** feel, but you could also make the frame in hot or acid colours for a very different result.

Be very careful when cutting mirror tiles as they produce small, sharp slivers of glass which should be swept up immediately and disposed of safely. Always wear protective leather gloves when handling cut tiles. The mirror tiles are set back from the edge of the frame so that you can safely grout over the cut edges. The mirror tiles could be replaced with border tiles in a strong colour, if desired.

MATERIALS

- Glazed ceramic floor tile insets: pale pink, white and black
- 1 cm (½ in) MDF (medium density fibreboard) or plywood
- Workbench and clamps
- Protective face mask
- Saw
- Protective leather gloves
- Safety goggles
- Wall tile cutter
- Mirror tiles
- Mirror tile adhesive pads
- Mirror, with polished edges
- Rubber gloves
- Flexible, cement-based tile adhesive
- Notched spreader
- Small plastic spatula
- Ready-mixed tile grout
- Sponge
- Lint-free cloth
- Closed-link metal chain and D-rings

1 Lay out the tiles on the backing. Decide the size of the frame, allowing for the mirror tile border and for grouting between each tile. Clamp the board and cut it to size, wearing a face mask.

2 Wearing protective leather gloves and goggles, use a tile cutter to cut the mirror tiles into 2.5 cm (1 in) wide strips.

3 Attach mirror tile pads every 8 cm (3 in) around the edges of the back of the mirror. Peel off the backing paper and fix the mirror in the centre of the frame.

4 Wearing rubber gloves, spread tile adhesive over the top section of the frame. Key (scuff) the surface with the notched edge of the spreader to ensure the tiles will adhere.

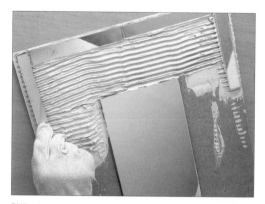

5 Wearing protective leather gloves, place strips of mirror tile around the outside edge of the frame, to within 6 mm ($\frac{1}{4}$ in) of the edge.

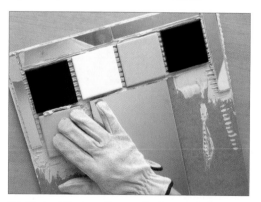

6 Set the inset tiles in position, spacing them evenly. Repeat steps 4 and 5 to complete the rest of the frame.

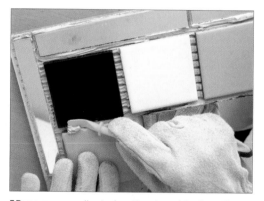

7 Remove excess adhesive from the edges of the tiles with a small spatula. Leave the frame to dry thoroughly.

8 Grout the frame, pushing the grout firmly between the tiles. Take care to cover the cut edges of the mirror tiles completely. Remove excess grout with a damp sponge, then polish the tiles with a dry, lint-free cloth. Firmly attach a strong, closed-link metal chain to the back of the frame for hanging.

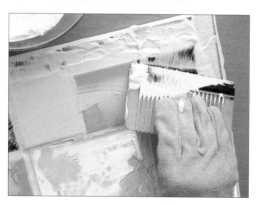

Black and White Tiled Table

Black and white tiled paths, porches and hallways are a familiar sight in town houses and they prove the age-old design theory that simplicity is best. There is something immensely pleasing about the simple regularity of black and white patterns, whether the tiles are set checkerboard style or as diamonds. There are many possible variations on the design shown here; the border could be made thicker or set out in one colour only. It should be noted that these tiles are not the heavy tessellated flooring, but a lighter variety that are easy to cut manually.

MATERIALS

- Small occasional table
- Diluted PVA (white) glue and brush
- Craft knife
- Pencil and ruler
- Protective face mask
- Hand saw
- Thin wooden batten
- Panel pins (tacks)
- Wood glue
- Tack hammer
- Protective leather gloves and goggles
- Tile cutter
- Small tiles in black and white
- Rubber gloves
- Notched spreader
- All-in-one flexible tile adhesive and grout
- Sponge
- Emulsion (latex) paint

1 Seal the top and bottom of the table top with a coat of diluted PVA (white) glue. When the wood has dried, key (scuff) the surface using a craft knife.

2 To help you to centre the tiles and work out how wide the borders will be, draw dividing lines as shown on the table top.

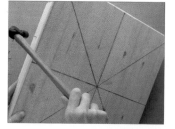

3 Wearing a protective face mask, cut four lengths of wooden batten to fit around the edges of the table. Attach with wood glue and panel pins, leaving a lip exactly the depth of the tiles at the top edge.

4 Wearing protective leather gloves and goggles, cut a few tiles diagonally to make triangles. Lay these out as a border on the table top and fill in with whole tiles to see how many will fit. Draw border lines around the edges.

5 Wearing rubber gloves, spread tile adhesive over the surface of the table top, inside the border lines. Starting with the triangular border tiles, set out the pattern, butting the tiles together and leaving very small gaps for grouting.

6 Wearing protective leather gloves and goggles, cut strips of tile to fit around the borders, then fix in place as before. Once the tiles have dried, grout the surface, removing any excess with a damp sponge. Seal and paint the table if required.

Decorative Planter

Embellish plain window boxes with pieces of tile, further enhanced by mixing a little cement dye into the grout to complement the colours of the tile pieces. Ensure the terracotta window box is frost resistant. If it has been designed specifically for outdoor use it is likely to withstand the most inclement weather.

MATERIALS

- Plain tiles in several colours
- Tile nippers
- Safety goggles
- Protective gloves
- Rubber gloves
- Notched spreader
- Waterproof tile adhesive
- Terracotta window box
- Putty knife
- Face mask
- Powdered waterproof tile grout
- Cement dye
- Mixing container
- Rubber spreader
- Nail brush
- Lint-free cloth

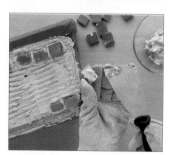

1 Snip the tiles into small pieces, wearing safety goggles and protective gloves. You will need a selection of small squares of a single colour and random shapes in several different colours. Wearing rubber gloves, use the notched spreader to apply tile adhesive to the sides of the planter.

2 Using a putty knife, apply a small amount of tile adhesive to a piece of broken tile. Position in place on the window box to form a border top and bottom.

3 Fill in the central design using the random tile shapes, mixing colours to make an abstract design. Apply small amounts of tile adhesive to the back of each piece as before. Leave fairly large gaps of a consistent size between the tile pieces, as thick bands of coloured grout are part of the final design. Leave to dry for 24 hours.

4 Wearing a protective face mask, goggles and rubber gloves, mix powdered grout with water and a little cement dye. Wearing gloves and using the rubber spreader, apply grout all over the surface of the window box, pressing right down between the tile pieces. Wipe the spreader over the surface of the window box to make sure the grout is evenly applied. Allow the surface to dry.

5 Brush off any excess grout with a nail brush, then leave to dry for 48 hours. Polish with a dry, lint-free cloth.

Plant Pots

For these delightful plant pots, fragments of plain and patterned broken tile have been incorporated into an overall design. Collect your materials by looking in junk shops and flea markets for old crockery in contrasting and complementary patterns. If the pots are intended to stand outside all through the year, be sure to use a frost-resistant terracotta pot as the base. If this is not available, a non-frost-resistant pot may be used, as long as it is waterproofed inside and out with a coat of **PVA (white) glue.**

MATERIALS
- Terracotta flower pots
- PVA (white) glue and brush (optional)
- Mixing container
- Acrylic paint
- Household paintbrush
- Chalk or wax crayon
- Plain and patterned tiles
- Safety goggles
- Protective gloves
- Tile nippers
- Rubber gloves
- Flexible knife
- Tile adhesive
- Face mask
- Powdered waterproof tile grout and cement dye
- Nail brush
- Lint-free cloth

1 If the plant pots are not frost-resistant and they are intended for outdoor use, treat inside and out by sealing with a coat of diluted PVA (white) glue. Allow to dry.

2 Paint the inside of the pots with acrylic paint in your chosen colour. Leave to dry.

3 Using chalk or a wax crayon, roughly sketch out the design for the tile pieces.

4 Wearing safety goggles and protective gloves, snip small pieces of tile to fit within your design. Wearing rubber gloves and using a flexible knife, spread tile adhesive on to small areas of the design at a time. Press tile pieces in place, working on the outlines first, then filling in background. Leave to dry for 24 hours.

5 Wearing a face mask and safety goggles, mix powdered grout with water and a little cement dye. Wearing rubber gloves, spread the grout over the pot, filling all the cracks between the tile pieces. Allow the surface to dry thoroughly.

6 Wearing a face mask and safety goggles, brush off any excess with a nail brush. Allow to dry thoroughly for at least 48 hours. Polish with a dry, soft cloth.

BASIC
TECHNIQUES

Decorative tiling is relatively straightforward and does not require a lot of expensive equipment. It pays to plan each tiling project carefully. Tiling the walls of a whole room is a large undertaking for a beginner but, the more you practise, the more skilled you will become. Projects such as a splashback or window recess can be accomplished after a little experience but certain rules will ensure success. It is important to prepare the surface to be tiled so that the tiles will adhere well. Tiles are simply too heavy to be applied on top of wallpaper or flaking paint. You must also use the correct tools – these are not difficult to get hold of but you cannot get away with using substitutes.

MATERIALS

Ceramic wall tiles Glazed wall tiles are waterproof and hardwearing, though brittle. They are thinner than floor tiles, usually about 6 mm (¼ in) thick, and come in a huge range of colours, sizes, designs and finishes. "Universal" tiles have four glazed edges, others have one, two or three glazed edges. Universal tiles may be used anywhere in a row of tiles, including edges and corners; the others are designed to finish off edges as appropriate. Tile borders are narrow strips used to edge a tiled area or to break it up. Some tiles have built-in spacers known as "lugs" that extend from the sides of the tiles, allowing regular spaces to be left for grouting.

Cold-set ceramic paints Non-toxic, water-based, cold-set ceramic paints are recommended for painting tiles. They are available in a wide range of colours and can be mixed or thinned with water. The paints set to a very durable finish after 48-72 hours but they are not as durable as unpainted glazed tiles. Care must be taken when grouting – keep the grout to the edges of the tile only. Do not clean the tiles vigorously, but wipe them with a damp cloth. If more permanent decoration is required, heat-fixable paints that are set in a domestic oven are available. Make sure your tiles are sturdy enough to be heated in this way.

Masking tape This removable paper tape is available in different widths. It is used to mask off areas to be painted, and also to hold stencils and tracings in place.

Mosaic tiles These are small tiles, sometimes with shaped insets, made of vitreous glass or glazed ceramic, usually sold in sheets on backing. Glass mosaic tiles are used for walls and pools, while ceramic tiles are used on floors or walls, depending on their strength.

Oiled stencil card (cardboard) This manilla-coloured card is impregnated with oil and comes in several gauges. Durable and water-resistant, it makes strong stencils with crisp edges that are easy to cut with a craft knife.

Powdered grout and grout colourant This is more economical than ready-mixed grout. Mix it with water to a creamy paste, following the manufacturer's instructions. Powdered grout comes in different colours

Right: Materials include: vinyl floor tiles (1); ceramic wall tiles (2), (3); mosaic tiles (4); powdered grout (5); cold-set ceramic paints (6); tube lining (7); masking tape (8); oiled stencil card (cardboard) (9); PVA (white) glue (10); waterproof all-in-one tile adhesive and grout (11); vinyl floor tile adhesive (12); grout colourant (13).

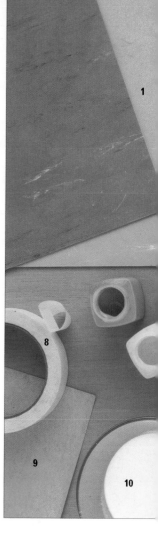

or can be coloured with grout colourant. Wear a protective face mask, safety goggles and rubber gloves when handling or mixing powdered materials.

PVA (white) glue Diluted PVA glue is used to seal porous surfaces such as plywood before tiling. It is also used to attach mosaic tesserae to backing paper when tiling by the "indirect" method as it dissolves in water.

Tube-lining This is used to draw a raised outline on the tile which can then be filled in with ceramic paints.

Vinyl floor tiles These thin, durable plastic tiles come in a wide range of colours and are ideal for checked patterns

and complicated tessellated floor designs. They are easy to score with a craft knife and snap by hand. They should be laid on a flat, smooth sub-floor such as hardboard – if they are laid directly on the floor they will show every bump and eventually crack. Some vinyl tiles are self-adhesive, with a paper backing; others are attached using a special adhesive, which must be used in a well-ventilated area. Vinyl tiles do not need grouting.

Vinyl floor tile adhesive Use this if the vinyl tiles you are using are not self-adhesive. Spread it thinly over the sub-floor using a fine-toothed notched spreader. Lay the

tiles as closely together as possible as they will not need grouting. Vinyl adhesive is very sticky, so if you make a mistake pull up the tile immediately and re-lay it before the glue sets. Always wear rubber gloves and work in a well-ventilated area when working with this adhesive.

Waterproof all-in-one tile adhesive and grout This thick white or coloured ready-mixed paste is used to fix and grout wall tiles. It is very easy to use and more convenient than separate adhesive and powdered grout. Always wear rubber gloves. Use flexible tile adhesive to tile a non-fixed surface such as wood or board.

EQUIPMENT

Craft knife Craft knives are very useful for making clean, precise cuts. Always cut away from your body and use a metal ruler to cut against.

Cutting mat This has a rubber surface. Use to protect your work surface when using a craft knife.

Flexible spreader Use this to "butter" extra tile adhesive on the back of irregular-shaped pieces of tile.

Hand-held tile cutters These plier-like tools are made in metal or plastic. They are equipped with a small diamond or tungsten carbide wheel that is strong enough to score the glazed surface of the tile. Always wear protective leather gloves and goggles when using.

Heavy sacking When breaking tiles with a hammer, wrap each tile in sacking first.

Lint-free cloth Ideal for polishing tiles after grouting.

Metal ruler A long metal ruler is very useful for marking out walls before tiling, measuring grids on floors, etc. Use a short metal ruler to cut against.

Mosaic nippers These strong-jawed pliers are used to cut glass tesserae to size and to shape ceramic tiles. Sharp shards of glass and china fly off when the tesserae and tiles are cut so always wear safety goggles and protective leather gloves.

Notched spreader This is used to spread tile adhesive. The notches make grooves in the adhesive that provide a "key" (scuffed surface) so that the tiles grip better.

Old saucer An old white china saucer is very useful for mixing paints. Do not use a paint saucer for food.

Paintbrushes A wide selection of brushes is useful but not essential. Try to have at least three sizes – thick, medium and fine – for varying brushstrokes.

Protective face mask and safety goggles These should always be worn for activities that produce dust, such as sawing and sanding wood or MDF (medium-density fibreboard), or cutting and smoothing tiles. They should also be worn when handling powdered materials.

Protective leather gloves These gloves are made of heavy suede and protect the hands and wrists. They should always be worn to protect your hands when cutting tiles or tesserae, or handling cut tiles.

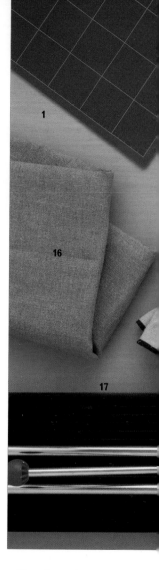

Right: *Useful equipment includes: self-healing cutting mat (1); craft knife (2); old saucer and paintbrushes (3); mosaic nippers (4); tile file (5); tack hammer (6); tile spacers (7); metal ruler (8); sponge (9); notched spreader (10); flexible spreader (11); spirit level (carpenter's level (12); hand-held tile cutters (13); set square (T-square) (14); protective leather gloves (15); heavy sacking (16); tile-cutting machine (17); protective face mask (18); safety goggles (19); lint-free cloth (20); rubber gloves (21).*

Rubber gloves Heavyweight rubber gloves should be worn when using tile adhesive, grout and grout colourant. If your skin is particularly sensitive, use a barrier cream also.

Set square (T-square) This is indispensable for aligning guide battens and checking that each row of tiles is straight.

Spirit level (carpenter's level) This will ensure a straight line when you are fixing a guide batten.

Sponge Use a damp sponge to remove excess tile adhesive and grout from tiles before it sets.

Tack hammer This lightweight hammer is ideal for knocking in panel pins (tacks). It is also good for breaking tiles to make pieces for mosaic work.

Tile file A broad file coated with tungsten carbide grit, used to smooth the edges of tiles before they are fixed in position. A lot of fine dust is produced, so always wear a dust mask, safety goggles and protective leather gloves.

Tile spacers These are small plastic crosses that are placed between tiles to create regular gaps for grouting. They are useful if you are using tiles without inbuilt spacer lugs. Some spacers are removed before grouting after the adhesive has dried. Others are much thinner and can be left in place and simply grouted over.

Tile-cutting machine For tiling a large area, a lightweight machine is more practical and less tiring than a hand-held tile cutter Wear protective goggles.

PREPARATION

Successful tiling, like many decorating techniques is dependent on how well you prepare the surface. The following methods will help you to make sure that you achieve an impressive and professional finish in your tiling project, whether it's a whole wall you are covering or a small area. It is worth taking time and care to perform these stages properly, otherwise you could be wasting a lot more time, and money, correcting mistakes. It is also a good idea to purchase or borrow the correct tools.

Tiling a Wall

1 Remove wallpaper or flaking paint from the wall. Fill cracks and holes. Leave new plaster to dry for 4 weeks and seal before tiling. Wash emulsion (latex) paint down with sugar soap then sand, wearing a protective face mask, to provide a key (scuffed surface) for the tiles.

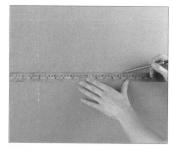

2 Calculate the number of tiles before you begin. Using a long metal ruler or metal tape measure, first find the centre of the wall. You usually need to cut some tiles to fit the wall. Set the cut tiles in the corners or at the edges of walls, where they will be least noticeable.

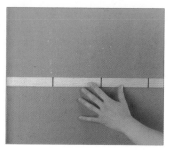

3 Mark a wooden strip with divisions one tile wide plus 2 mm ($\frac{1}{16}$ in) either side. Place in the centre of the wall, holding it vertically, then horizontally. If the edges of the wall fall between two divisions on the strip, you can see the width of the cut tiles needed.

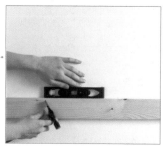

4 Wall tiles should be applied upwards from a measured baseline, usually one tile up from a skirting board (base board), sink or the side of a bath. First draw the baseline, then attach a wooden batten with the top edge along the line. Hammer the nails in only part-way. Check with a spirit level (carpenter's level).

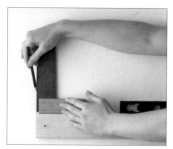

5 Use a plumbline to establish a true vertical at the side of the batten. Using a set square (T-square), draw a second line at this point to mark the side edge of the first complete tile in each row. Attach a batten along the outside of the line.

6 Wearing rubber gloves, spread a thin layer of tile adhesive (approximately 3 mm ($\frac{1}{8}$ in) deep) over the wall, inside the battens. Only cover a small area at a time, otherwise the adhesive will dry before you have time to tile it.

7 Using the notched edge of the spreader, "comb" the adhesive to key (scuff) the surface so that the tiles will adhere well. If you do not provide a good surface, the finished result will be less successful.

8 Starting in the bottom corner, lay the first tile. Push it into position with a slight twisting movement to cover the back of the tile with adhesive.

9 Some tiles have built-in spacer lugs. If not, use plastic spacers at the corners of the tiles so that the grouting lines are regular. Some spacers are removed before grouting, others are very thin and can be grouted over. Remove excess adhesive with a damp sponge before it hardens. Check the tiles' straightness with a spirit level every few rows, and adjust as necessary.

10 When the tile adhesive is dry, remove the battens. Add cut tiles at the edges of the tiled area if necessary. Leave for about 24 hours. Using the rubber edge of the spreader, apply grout to the gaps between the tiles. It is important to use the right grout depending on where the tiles are used. Make sure the gaps are completely filled, or small holes known as "pinholing" will appear as it dries.

11 When the grout has hardened slightly, pull a rounded stick down the gaps between the tiles to give a smooth finish to the grout. Add a little more grout if there are any pinholes.

12 Leave the grout to set for about 30 minutes, then remove the excess with a damp sponge. When the grout is completely dry, polish the surface of the tiles with a dry, lint-free cloth.

Cutting Tiles

1 To use a hand-held tile cutter, measure the width required and deduct 2 mm ($\frac{1}{16}$ in) to allow for grouting. Mark the cutting line on the tile. Place the cutting wheel against a short metal ruler and score down the line once only to pierce the glaze.

2 Wearing protective leather gloves and safety goggles, place the tile as far as it will go into the jaws of the cutter with the scored line positioned centrally. Close the handles of the cutter to snap the tile in two.

3 Manual cutting machines will cut tiles up to about 6 mm ($\frac{1}{4}$ in) thick quickly and accurately, and they have a useful measuring gauge. Adjust the gauge to the right width and pull the wheel once down the tile to score a cutting line. Remove the tile and snap along this line.

4 Wearing protective leather gloves, a face mask and safety goggles, use a tile file to smooth the cut edge of the tile if desired.

Tile Mosaic

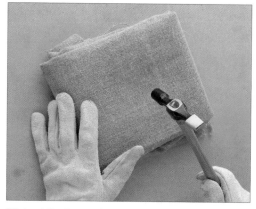

1 Mosaic tesserae and small pieces of tile can be shaped with mosaic nippers. Wearing protective leather gloves and safety goggles, place the jaws of the nippers at right angles to the tile and press them together to make a clean cut. Clear away small, sharp shards of tile immediately and dispose of them safely.

2 To break tiles for mosaics, wrap each tile separately in several layers of heavy sacking and place on a wooden cutting board. Wearing protective leather gloves and safety goggles, tap the tile smartly several times with a hammer. Unwrap carefully and dispose immediately of small, unusable shards.

Powdered Grout

1 When mixing up powdered grout, add the powder to a measured amount of water, rather than the other way round, otherwise the mixture may be lumpy. Mix the powder thoroughly into the water. Always wear rubber gloves, a protective face mask and safety goggles when mixing powdered grout.

2 Grout colourant can be added to the powdered grout before mixing it with water. Wear protective clothing as for powdered grout, and mix with water in the proportion advised by the manufacturer.

To Remove Grease

1 You may wish to decorate tiles that are not in pristine condition. It is essential to start with a clean surface to ensure an even application of paint. To remove grease and fingerprints from the surface of tiles before painting, wipe them over with a weak solution of 1 part malt vinegar to 10 parts water.

To Transfer a Design

1 To transfer a design on to a tile, cut a piece of tracing paper the same size as the tile. Trace the design, making sure it is positioned centrally, then place the paper face down on the tile, matching the edges. Scribble over the lines to transfer them to the tile. If the design is not symmetrical, scribble over the lines before placing the paper on the tile. Position the tracing face up on the tile and redraw over the original lines.

TEMPLATES

The templates on these pages have been produced at a percentage of their actual size. To enlarge the templates, you can either use a photocopier or a grid system. Once you have enlarged the design on a photocopier, trace and transfer on to the tile as described earlier in this section. To use the grid system to enlarge your design, draw a grid of evenly spaced squares over the image. On a second piece of paper draw a larger grid, and copy the original design, square by square into the larger grid to complete your design. Finally, draw over the design to make sure all the lines are continuous and trace and transfer on to the tile as before.

Fish Tiles p85

Cactus Tiles p84

Daisy Tiles p86

Cartoon Tiles p83

Stamp Tiles p90

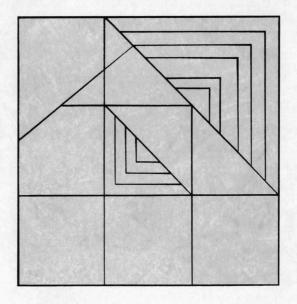

Art Deco Tiles p92-3

Art Nouveau Tiles p94-5

Mexican Animal Tiles p81

Seaside Tiles p91

Seaside Tiles p91

Heraldic Dragon Tiles p96

Persian Carnation Tiles p97

Majolica Tiles p98

Medieval Tiles p99

Byzantine Bird Tile p102

William Morris Tiles p100-1

ACKNOWLEDGEMENTS

AUTHOR'S ACKNOWLEDGEMENTS

There are many people I would like to thank for making this book possible. In particular, Lindsay Porter, whose tireless enthusiasm, creativity and sense of humour made the project a real pleasure; Adrian Taylor and his assistant, James Arnold whose photography and styling resulted in such wonderful pictures; Neil Hadfield for his creative contribution and for driving me to so many tile warehouses; Clare Hunt for finding such beautiful objects and Sandra Hadfield for all her help in the studio. I am also grateful to craftspeople, tile gallery owners and tile manufacturers who so generously loaned items for photography, and all the contributors for their hard work and creativity.

The author and publishers would like to thank the following for creating the projects for this book:

Helen Baird: pp116-18, pp126-7, pp128-130; Evelyn Bennett: p91, p103; Petra Boase: p72, p73; Mary Fellows: p68, p69, p70, p83; Lucinda Ganderton: pp92-3, p94, p96, p97, p98, p99, pp100-1, p102; Sandra Hadfield: pp120-2, pp123-5, pp131-3, pp136-7; Francesca Kaye: p80, p82; Cleo Mussi: pp138-9; Christopher New: p81, pp112-15; Marie Perkins: p84, p85, p86

The following generously lent transparencies or tiles for photography:

Artiles, Fired Earth Tile Co.
218 Madras Street, PO Box 22-647
Christchurch, New Zealand

Candy Tiles
Great Western Potteries
Heathfield, Newton Abbot TQ12 6RS
England

Ceramica Blue
10 Blenheim Crescent
London W11 1NN
England

Cosmo Place Studio
11 Cosmo Place
London WC1N 3AP

Elon Tiles Ltd
66 Fulham Road
London SW3 6HH

Fired Earth Plc
Twyford Mill
Oxford Road
Adderbury
Oxon OX17 3HP

H & R Johnson Ltd
Highgate Tile Works
Tunstall
Stoke-on-Trent ST6 4JX

The Kasbah
8 Southampton Place
London WC2E 7HA

Life Enhancing Tile Co.
31 Bath Buildings
Montpelier
Bristol BS6 5PT

Mosaic Workshop
443 Holloway Road
London N7 6LJ

Mosaïk
10 Kensington Square
London W8 5EP

Original Style Ltd
Falcon Road
Sowton Industrial Estate
Exeter EX2 7LF

Paris Ceramics
583 Kings Road
London SW6 2EH

Terra Firma Tiles
70 Chalk Farm Road
London NW1 8AN
England

The Tile Gallery
1 Royal Parade
247 Dawes Road

London SW6 7RE
England

The Tile Heritage Foundation
P O Box 1850 Healdsburg
CA 95448
USA

Victoria and Albert Museum
Cromwell Road
London SW7 2RL

PICTURE CREDITS

The publishers and author would like to thank the following for additional photography: Ancient Art and Architecture Collection Ltd: p16 br and bl; Sylvia Cordaiy Photo Library: p19 tl, p21 b, p108 t, p108 b; Edifice: p10 tl, p13 br, p18 b, p19 tl, p20 bl, p27 l, p28 b, p29 John Freeman: p13 t, p26 bl, p26 br, p28 r, p39 br; Michelle Garrett: p36 b, p38 tr, p65b; Hearst Castle: p32 t, p33 t; John Heseltine: p12 t, p12 bl, p21 t; Tim Imrie: p39 bl, p111; Jayawadene Photo Library: p6 tl, p8, p12 bl, p14 b, p15; Liverpool City Museum: p24 t; Malibu Lagoon Museum: p33 b; Gloria Nicol: p65 br; Debbie Patterson: p4 br, p36 t, p37 b, p64 bl, p109b, p110 bl Graham Rae: p39 t, p40-41, p110tl; Spike Powell: p5 tr, p110 tr; Tile Heritage Foundation: p 33 br; Victoria and Albert Picture Library: p11 t, p22 bl, p22 br, p23, p24b, p25, p26 t, p27 l, p31 l; Andy Williams: p17.

INDEX

BIBLIOGRAPHY

Arts and Crafts in Britain and America, Isabelle Anscombe and Charlotte Gere, Academy Editions 1978
The Decorative Tile, Tony Herbert and Kathryn Higgins, Phaidon Press 1995
Dictionary of Islamic Architecture, Andrew Peterson, Routledge 1996
The Edwardian House, Helen Long, Manchester University Press 1993
A Guide to the Collection of Tiles in the Victoria and Albert Museum, Arthur Lane 1939
Handmade Tiles, Frank Giorgini, David and Charles 1994
Islamic Art, David Talbot Rice, Thames and Hudson 1975
Islamic Tiles, Venetia Porter, British Museum Press 1995
Liverpool Pottery, Alan Smith, City of Liverpool Museums

Pottery and Ceramics, Ernst Rosenthal, Pelican Books 1949
Pottery Through the Ages, George Savage, Pelican Books 1959
Suburban Style, Helena Barrett and John Phillips, Macdonald Orbis 1987
Temples, Churches and Mosques, J.G. Davies, Basil Blackwell 1992
Tile, Jill Herber, Artisan 1996
Tiles in Architecture, Hans Van Leeman, Laurence King Publishing 1993
Tiles, a Collector's Guide, Hans Van Leemen, Souvenir Press 1979
Victorian Architecture, Roger Dixon and Stefan Muthesius, Thames and Hudson 1993
The Victorian House, John Marshall and Ian Willox, Sidgwick and Jackson 1986